D0645710

Rebecca Florence Osaigbovo

chosen
vessels

◆◆◆◆◆◆◆◆◆◆◆◆◆◆◆◆◆◆◆◆◆◆◆◆◆◆

women of color ◆ keys to change

Foreword by John M. Perkins

InterVarsity Press
Downers Grove, Illinois

InterVarsity Press
P.O. Box 1400, Downers Grove, IL 60515-1426
World Wide Web: www.ivpress.com
E-mail: mail@ivpress.com

InterVarsity Press® is the book-publishing division of InterVarsity Christian Fellowship/USA®, a
student movement active on campus at hundreds of universities, colleges and schools of nursing in
the United States of America, and a member movement of the International Fellowship of
Evangelical Students. For information about local and regional activities, write Public Relations
Dept., InterVarsity Christian Fellowship/USA, 6400 Schroeder Rd., P.O. Box 7895, Madison, WI
53707-7895, or visit the IVCF website at <www.ivcf.org>.

Cover photograph: Pam Rice

ISBN 0-8308-2380-8

Printed in the United States of America ∞

Library of Congress Cataloging-in-Publication Data

Osaigbovo, Rebecca
  Chosen vessels: women of color, keys to change / Rebecca Florence
Osaigbovo; foreword by John M. Perkins.
    p. cm.
  ISBN 0-8308-2380-8 (pbk. : alk. paper)
1. African American women—Religious life. I. Title.
BR563.N4 083 2002
277.3'0082—dc21

                                                                        2002004049

P 17 16 15 14 13 12 11 10 9 8 7 6 5 4 3 2 1

Y 15 14 13 12 11 10 09 08 07 06 05 04 03 02

contents

◆ ◆ ◆ ◆ ◆

Part 4: The Healing Process

Part 5: Let the Change Begin

foreword

◆ ◆ ◆ ◆ ◆ ◆

Rebecca Osaigbovo has broken the long silence of African American women. Over the years we have heard millions of voices babbling about the state of the black woman. People (primarily men) offer their theological opinion on the subject; radical feminists have even thrown in their two cents worth. Everyone in our society is telling the black woman what she should do. The question arises, who should she listen to?

In *Chosen Vessels: Women of Color, Keys to Change* we finally hear a voice from the inside—the voice of an African American woman speaking to other African American women. In this book Rebecca provides a road other women can follow in helping to restore the black family to a biblical foundation. In our current society, the black woman must find healing in order to be empowered to regain a positive role in her family. In this way, both she and her family can profoundly and positively affect American society.

Unfortunately, some of our young black males—perhaps out of frustration—have turned against black females and are brutalizing them verbally, emotionally and physically. This book gives examples of a biblical standard that can be adhered to in the midst of this abuse and degradation.

Rebecca speaks out in defense of a biblical view of the American black woman. *Chosen Vessels* will help to change the way black women see themselves and the way they are viewed by society. It will also help affirm our dignity as a people. This book is timely and so needed at this time when more and more of our families are broken and many headed by females.

Chosen Vessels is not just a book for African American women. It goes further than that; it deals with the great issues that are so prevalent in the day in which we are living—ones which our society as a whole needs to hear. This book should be exposed to all other ethnic groups as well as to every African American family.

Rebecca, I commend you for taking a strong and noble stand in this critical time in the history of our people. I commend you for setting a theological view for women of color. May God richly bless you and may this book be received greatly throughout all our nation.

John Perkins

preface

◆ ◆ ◆ ◆ ◆

"May I speak to Rebecca . . . I'll probably murder this last name."

"That's okay. It's O-sig'-bo-vo. This is Rebecca."

"This is Rebecca? Oh, Rebecca. My name is . . . . I'm calling from Texas. Girl, I have read *Chosen Vessels*. It is such a good book. That book is for everyone. Have you ever considered writing this book for all women? I'm African American myself. But I know a whole lot of other people who could really benefit from this book. I really think you need to consider writing it differently. You could sell so many more books if you did that."

Fubu

I have been encouraged over the last nine years to position this book so that it would have greater appeal to people other than African American women. I've been told that its content would be good for all women and men. I seriously considered making the book appeal to everybody, especially as I was contemplating writing this revised edition of *Chosen Vessels*.

It certainly would have made more economic sense, but I really felt God wanted to talk specifically to us (African American women) by us (an African American female author) through this book. I have to go with my heart, not my head. I want to say up front that this book remains fubu (for us by us).[1]

Although there is a broader audience who would benefit by reading the content, I cannot change the focus of the book to give it uni-

---

[1]Fubu is a contemporary African American clothing company.

versal appeal. To do that would dilute its purpose of confronting the lies African American Christian women believe so they can be free to be all God wants. African American Christian women need to know that as much as God loves everyone else, he knows their unique plight and has a specific message for them. I believe that is God's goal.

That is not to say that *Chosen Vessels* should be restricted reading for someone who is not an African American Christian woman. In these days it's hard to find many who did not come from a dysfunctional family or experience some type of abuse, rejection or major disappointment. Many people other than African American women will be able to identify with some of what we will discuss in this book. You don't have to be embarrassed about passing this book along to others.

Issues that all women can relate to are addressed within the pages of this book. African American males and others who have experienced rejection due to a physical characteristic beyond their control—an accent, one's skin tone or a handicap—will also be able to identify with some of what I say about the African American's plight.

I thank God for using the self-published edition of *Chosen Vessels* to transform the lives of many black women. I just received a letter from a lady who said, "I read your book *Chosen Vessels* years ago and was tremendously blessed by it. I went on to share your book with many hurting women who have since been delivered from situations they were battling."

The most common comment we received was, "This is a book every black woman should read." Over sixty thousand copies of the first edition were sold, and no telling how many women read the book. However, if every black Christian woman could benefit from this book, we still have a ways to go. I pray with this refocused revised edition, and along with our partner InterVarsity Press, we can come closer to realizing that outcome.

Still, I do believe this is an important book for every member of the church of Jesus Christ in this country. Those who are genuinely concerned for all members of the body of Christ coming into oneness need to understand the plight of African American Christian women. Certainly if someone is in any way related to an African American Christian woman (including someone they work with, worship with or want to minister to), then by all means they can glean what they can about us from this book. I trust they will use the insights gained to pray for us. I hope they will ask God how he might want to use them in facilitating oneness among all the people of God. It is my desire that they would recommend this book to others so that more would begin to understand the pivotal role African American Christian women have in the kingdom of God.

And as they listen in on our discussion, they shouldn't be surprised if they get ministered to in the process.

Using This Book
This book is designed to facilitate growth. At the end of each chapter there are questions for individual or group study. These questions pull out additional biblical principles, help you to apply what you are reading to your life and show you how to pray for healing. Each chapter has a challenge question designed for individuals to go deeper into the themes. Overall you will get the most out of the book if you work through the material on your own and then discuss it with a group. You will be able to pray for each other, challenge each other to grow and encourage each other with your insights.

In this book I like to make the case that the Holy Spirit's work among African American Christian women is pivotal in the purposes of God of making the church glorious. Furthermore I believe African American Christian women are the keys to change for this whole nation.

This may seem far-fetched, but I actually believe that much of what God wants to do in this nation is contingent upon African American Christian women. In other words, the church of Jesus Christ in America is not going to progress much further in God's purposes until African American Christians take their place. I trust this book will facilitate that happening.

I believe God used the original edition of *Chosen Vessels* to speak a message he wanted many of us to hear. It still amazes me that he chose me as the vessel to deliver that message to African American women. So many times I've needed the message myself.

Just recently I was talking to a friend, and we were discussing how messed up we both were and really just praising God for being as great and mighty as he is to be able to use broken vessels (or cracked pots) such as us. We have a saying that we find ourselves repeating over and over: "It's not about us."

Thank God, it's not about us. It's about a big God who is bigger than our problems, past mistakes, weakness and faults. He is greater than our sins. And it is to him that all credit belongs. The essence of the message of this book is, God has chosen to use you, African American Christian woman . . . in spite of you.

part 1
african american women

1

african american women: chosen vessels

• •

But God has chosen the foolish things of the world to put to shame the wise, and God has chosen the weak things of the world to put to shame the things which are mighty; and the base things of the world and the things which are despised God has chosen, and the things which are not, to bring to nothing things that are, that no flesh should glory in His presence. (1 CORINTHIANS 1:27-30)

I do not pray for these alone, but also for those who will believe in Me through their word; that they all may be one, as You, Father, are in Me, and I in You; that they also may be one in Us, that the world may believe that You sent Me. (JOHN 17:20-21, EMPHASIS ADDED)

There is much work God has to do among African American Christian women. For a variety of reasons many women of color do not feel they are a significant part of the whole. God desires *all* to be made one. I believe it is very difficult for many African American Christians to truly connect with other members of the whole because of protective walls around them. These walls are in place because of prior injury and rejection from other members of the whole.

That *All* May Be One

What happens to a corporate group when some members do not understand they are an important part of the whole? Discouragement, division, disconnection, despair, even defection can often result when members of a team or army do not "feel" they are important.

When there is an injury in our physical bodies, the blood will rush to that spot to begin the healing process. Because of the severity of the injury that many African American women have suffered, God has focused his attention there for the ultimate fulfillment of his purpose: bringing the whole into a unity of love (John 17).

Does that mean African American women are more important than other members of the body of Christ? No, I don't think it means that. I believe it means that African American Christian women need an abundant outpouring of God's grace and mercy in measures above what many others may need at this point to confront the lies they believe about themselves and to knock down the walls of separation.

A Little Personal Background

I may not have had the typical African American upbringing, if there is such a thing. I was born and raised in a small town in the South by parents who were missionaries. They served at Cedine Bible Mission, now called Cedine Ministries, in Spring City, Tennessee. But like many African American women I still had the questions: Do African American women have a place in God's purposes? Has God forgotten about us? How do I reconcile a God of love with many of our painful experiences?

Now, after living in two different metropolitan cities of the North, Chicago and Detroit; working in the field of substance abuse nursing for a number of years; and meeting and ministering to African American women locally and all over this country, the same questions keep coming up.

As I have asked these questions, I believe God has given me some answers. When I began to say to others what I thought God was saying to me, in some ways I was still trying to convince myself. This was new territory for me. The message appeared just a little on the edge. I struggled big time with my own esteem issues, wondering how God could ever use me. Even after it became clear he was using me, I still struggled with why he would use someone like myself who still had so many issues.

I am more convinced *now* than when I began writing this book ten years ago that African American women are the keys to change. I am convinced that God has specific plans for us and we have a critical part to play in God's overall purposes.

Equally, I am also more convinced *now* than ever that African American Christian women are the most unlikely candidates to be used by God. I discovered I'm more messed up than I knew I was. Fortunately I've also made the discovery it's about God and his ability to use us in spite of us.

We'll mention some of the issues African American women have, many which run deep and are in direct opposition to the ways of God. What gives me hope and a reason to be filled with praise and thanksgiving is that God is big enough to chose and use the most unlikely candidates. So I've learned to relax about my inadequacies. The Lord's purposes will prevail (Proverbs 19:21).

The purpose of God's Spirit in any group of people is the same: conforming individuals into the image of Jesus. However the actual process will be unique for different cultural groupings. This book considers the work God is doing and desires to continue among African American women.

Let me say here that in the realm of the Spirit, no racial or ethnic differences exist. The Spirit of God is the same inside of me as inside of a Christian man who lives in South America. Some of the Spirit's attributes are joy, kindness, patience, love, longsuffering and gentleness. However as the Spirit of God begins to grow me up so that his attributes are more visibly expressed in my life, he may have different obstacles to overcome as he works his way out into my behavior through the maturing process. The outworking of the Spirit of God inside of me to the natural realm is where the difference occurs. The spots and blemishes in my soul are different from those the South American young man or someone from another ethnic group might face.

God has a specific message for African American women. What is the thrust of that message? God wants to confront and root out deeply ingrained lies. He wants us to see ourselves as a significant part of his plan. God desires for us to be special recipients of his grace. We can then give of ourselves from that grace and be a force for change in the kingdom, and in the world.

It is time for African American women who may have felt left out of God's purposes to find out the special place reserved for them. God needs everyone to stand in the victory secured by Jesus! God is looking for a group of overcomers who will stand strong in the days we are living in.

God is not prejudiced. He does not love us more than anyone else, and he doesn't love everyone else more than us. Everyone can be in close partnership with God, knowing their God and doing exploits (Daniel 11:2). Everyone is called. But few are chosen. I believe that many African American women are destined to be chosen vessels. This means that not only are they called, but they are also chosen to participate with the heavenly Father in bringing his will on earth as it is in heaven.

Why would I say many of us are chosen vessels? I'll give two reasons. One is found in 1 Corinthians 1:26-28. African American women are often thought of as being the lowest. We have historically been on the bottom of the economic and social ladder. God says he chooses those whom the world considers foolish to confound the wise. I believe African American women are specifically called to be chosen vessels in God's hands because of our status in this country: on the bottom.

The second reason I believe African American women are called to be chosen vessels in God's hands in the times we are living in is because we have suffered much. I know many of us do not equate suffering with a significant call of God as a chosen vessel. But I want to take us to the place in the Word of God in which God specifically states that someone he chose as a vessel would have to suffer:

> But the LORD said to him, "Go, for he is a chosen vessel of Mine to bear My name before Gentiles, kings, and the children of Israel. For I will show him how many things he must suffer for My name's sake." (Acts 9:15-16)

The apostle Paul was a chosen vessel. He suffered much for the sake of Christ. I believe a lot of the suffering of African American women has been for the sake of Christ. We have not understood that. As a result, we have had many problems with the plight of our lives.

Like Esther, we have not understood that maybe we have been brought into the kingdom for such a time as this. We can gain insights from the lives of Paul and Esther found in Scripture. But I believe the biblical character we can gain the most insights from is Joseph. His story is found in the book of Genesis.

A parallel exists between African Americans and Joseph. Joseph, sold into slavery by his brothers, was a slave for a number of years. As a slave, he was lied about, put into prison and severely wronged. But God had a destiny for Joseph all along. And though Satan meant what happened to Joseph for evil, God intended it for good (Genesis 50:20).

Joseph's God-ordained destiny was to be in charge of keeping the Egyptians and others, especially his family who had already been chosen to become a nation of God's chosen people, alive during a time of severe famine. But first Joseph would have to suffer in the depths of his soul. God knew his hardship would produce in him a severe commitment to justice and equity in his eventual role as head of food distribution.

Joseph had to be responsive to the needs of all people, whether poor or not; he had to experience the pits of slavery, attacks on his character and imprisonment. All of his experiences worked compassion into him. It also served to uproot pride.

Joseph had a choice. He could choose to be bitter. But he could also choose to forgive those who sold him into slavery and those who abused him in Egypt. He chose the latter and became a hero in God's hall of fame.

Today there is another Joseph (or should we say Josephine) God has chosen for a destiny of greatness. Long ago this Josephine also dreamed of greatness, excelling in everything. Even after a period of slavery, people demeaned her character and abilities and put her into prison—the prisons of drugs, sex, violence, bitterness and religion.

In spite of all of that, this Josephine has survived the greatest odds. A dream is still in her spirit. God remembers the dream. He has not forgotten his purposes for her. Yes, Satan meant all of the injustices for us as African Americans, and particularly as African American women, for evil, but God had good in mind. God is ready to bring Josephine out of the prison and into the throne room, second to none as it relates to prayer.

As African American Christian women we, like Joseph, will now have to decide whether we will forgive others for the bitter experience of slavery, injustice and rejection or sink further into the abyss of bitterness and blame.

Our response at this critical time will determine whether we will remain in prison or move into the throne room of the kingdom of God. Our destiny is to be a force for change in God's kingdom, second to none in our relationship to our Father and in having his grace, favor, wisdom and power available to us and our loved ones.

As a people we have lived in the wilderness. We know the pitfalls of the wilderness. We have been forced to depend on Jesus alone. As a people in this nation, many times the only thing we have had to hang on to has been Jesus.

None of us knows how long it will be until Jesus returns. But Scripture indicates things will get worse and worse as we approach the last of the last days. African Americans have already gone through many of the rough times that may still be ahead for America. Those who depended upon God and even some who did not—survived. Who knows? We may be asked to lead others in America through the wilderness even as Moses' father-in-law and his people were asked to be eyes for the children of Israel (Numbers 10:29-31).

In the throne room close to the King, we have the opportunity to hear from him secrets, wisdom, perhaps answers to economic woes, drug addiction, AIDS, cancer, the environment—any number of problems. Second to none in the throne room, we can hear what God wants to do. Because of our confidence in God, we will ask him to do it. Then we'll sit back and watch him answer what he told us to ask and thereby work in a junior partnership with him as he accomplishes his purposes in the earth.

How do we get from where we are to where God wants us? Let me explain what I hope to accomplish in this book. First, I want to show the way it could be. In the very next chapter I want to begin to portray a vision of what I think is God's plan for us as African American Christian women by painting a picture of the future: the ultimate results of the outpouring of God's Spirit on us. Next, I'll tell it like it is. I have alluded to the fact that African American women have some issues. I don't like admitting it myself, but it's the truth anyhow. In chapter three I take a reality-check look at us.

How and why are we the way we are? Section two will go back to the beginning of time and examine the creation of mankind, look at the enemy of God and begin to explore the plans and ways of God's enemy. The way we are is the direct result of the attack of the enemy of God. So, sisters, we've got to go there. It won't be too spooky to handle; just some dry facts about beings you can't see—facts we have to explore if we want to understand what's been happening.

Section three will go into detail considering the specifics of the attack of the enemy against women and against African Americans that resulted in the double-whammy effect on African American women that we discussed in chapter three.

Section four will examine 2 Chronicles 7:14 as the recipe for getting out from under the enemy's plan and his hands into the hands of a faithful God as chosen vessels.

The book closes with help and admonition to make a change.

Come with me as we journey into the plans and purposes of God Almighty!

Questions for Thought and Action

1. Read 1 Corinthians 1:27-30 in your Bible, noting the surrounding context. Then read it in at least one other version or translation such as NIV, NLT, Amplified or NAS. Who wrote the passage? Who were the recipients of the passage? What light does that shed on how God uses the "foolish"?

2. Think of a time when you were in an interracial Christian setting. Was it difficult for you to connect? Identify some of your thoughts/emotions.

3. Read John 17:9-26. According to Jesus, why is it so important that Christians demonstrate oneness?

4. Which of the questions listed under the heading "A Little Personal Background" have you also struggled with?

5. The chapter says, "African American women are the most unlikely candidates to be used by God." What statement do you think God is trying to make when he chooses unlikely candidates?

6. How does the plight of African American females give them a potential advantage in knowing God?

7. *Going deeper:* Read the story of Joseph in Genesis 37—45. How is your life similar to Joseph's? (Have you ever been betrayed? Have you ever been a slave to food, cigarettes? Have you ever been in a literal or figurative prison? Have you personally been lied about on your job, in your family, in church or school? Have people ever promised you something and then forgotten you when they moved on?)

8. Take a moment now to meditate upon and pray aloud this prayer. (If you cannot pray it at this time, perhaps you will be able to at a later time.) "Father, I now ask you to forgive all who were involved from Africa, Europe and here in America in the slave trading of my ancestors. I ask you not to hold anything to their account. I release everyone involved."

2

a vision of hope for the future

◆ ◆

For I know the thoughts that I think toward you, says the LORD,
thoughts of peace and not of evil, to give you a future and a hope.
(JEREMIAH 29:11)

Do not remember the former things, nor consider the things of old.
Behold, I will do a new thing, Now it shall spring forth; Shall you not know it?
I will even make a road in the wilderness and rivers in the desert.
(ISAIAH 43:18-19)

One time my crazy cousin took care of my kids and he prayed over my house while I was gone. I poured my bottle of liquor down the toilet when I got home. I don't even know why I did it. . . . I wasn't even thinking about God before that. But soon I became more and more dissatisfied with my life and began the journey of returning to God."

The above incident actually happened. Linda Moore, a neighbor of mine when I first came to Detroit and now a friend, told me of this incident. She is actually a Christian today because of the prayers of her "crazy cousin." Can prayer really change people? Yes, I believe seeing prayers change things can be commonplace as African American women get close to God and become keys to change in his hands.

God can do such a work in us and in our loved ones that our past and present can be like a bad dream. If we really understood what God has in store for us, it would blow our minds. I believe God is poised right now to do a new thing, and as he does it we can expect to see real change in our families and communities and this nation.

A Cure for All Ills by Mary Relfe will give you a taste of what God has done and a thirst to see it happen again. In this book she chronicles past moves of God's Spirit that resulted in sweeping changes in society. There was a time in the 1800s that God's Spirit was so much at work in a community that policeman had to be laid off because they had run out of work to do. Saloons and houses of ill repute were closed, not because of marches or petitions, but because they lacked customers.

Just imagine the following conversations:

"Mom, I just called to tell you I'm starting to go back to church."

"Elise, I've spent a few months trying to find you. I just wanted to tell you I have recently become a Christian. I wanted to ask you to forgive me for how I treated you when you worked for me a few years ago. You really were the most qualified for that promotion and I was the one who made sure you did not get it. Now that I know the Lord, he has really been dealing with me about a lot of my messed up thinking. I know you were a Christian back then. I realize it might be hard to accept me as your new brother in the Lord. But I wanted you to know I'm a changed person, and I want to do what I can to make things right. By the way, did you pray for me like the Bible says we should do for our enemies? I've often thought you may have had something to do with my coming to know Jesus. Can we get together for lunch? I have so much to share, and I just want to thank you for showing me an example of Christ."

"Son, I want to apologize for the way I treated your mom during the years you were growing up. I know it wasn't a good example. I didn't know it then. I was doing what I was taught. I'm praying that God will help you follow his ways with your new wife."

"You know, I just can't get high. I've been using all night. I bet my mom has been praying again. We might as well stop and try again tomorrow. I'll just call her in the morning and upset her so she'll spend her day worrying instead of praying."

How would you like to read the paper or turn on the news and learn that crack houses and abortion clinics were closing due to a lack of customers? In times of refreshing from the Lord in the past, churches were packed and the news media was forced to acknowledge that change was taking place.

"This is Ted Koppel. Tonight we will go to New York, Detroit, Chicago, L.A., Atlanta and Washington, D.C., to examine a strange phenomenon. It appears some African American ladies have tapped into what they call the power of prayer. We are getting reports of 'revival' breaking out in our state prisons.

"Drug lords and the Mafia are upset; their profits have plunged in the last few months. They have a hard time even giving away crack cocaine.

"Payment of child support has been documented to be at an all time high. Tales of apologies and reconciliations abound. Stores all over this nation are reporting the return of stolen items. Folks, I don't know what this is. We have never seen anything like it before. Tune in tonight and we'll be interviewing a hard core prisoner serving time for murder. He says he has had this 'conversion' experience, something about his grandmother praying . . ."

How would you like to have your wayward child call you and tell you they are returning to God? What would it be like if some of the many people who abused, rejected or neglected you finally admitted their wrong to you? Would you like to see many of our men and women who have been incarcerated released because of the transforming work of God in their lives? They could come home stronger Christians than many in our churches.

(Hey, hey, hey, single sisters. If he's a new creation in Christ, he is new indeed. You've been praying, don't get no attitude. He just might be that gold God has kept locked up until such a time as this.)

In Ephesians 3:20 the apostle Paul says God "is able to do exceedingly abundantly above all that we ask or think according to the power that works in us." African American women can be keys to change as God's power is at work in us and through us.

That excites me! As I look at other women of color and even myself at times, it may seem as if we have no hope. Relationship problems, financial problems, health problems, time management problems, boss problems, loneliness problems, weight problems, clutter control problems, work problems, children problems, car problems . . . do I need to go on?

I won't lie to you and tell you it's going to be easy. African American Christian women will have to press really hard to break through the challenges and the lies in our own minds about our worth, God's love and other issues. But if we are willing to hang in there and allow God to remove the garbage in our minds, we can inherit freedom and the blessings of God on our lives and communities. It's because we have so many problems that we're in a key position to really experience God in a major way.

We won't be satisfied with our own freedom. It is extremely important to walk with God to destroy the works of the devil in the lives of our family, friends and fellow members in the family of God.

As African American women begin to walk in truth, we can begin to come out from under the curse of our past. We do not have to continue reacting the way we have been programmed. We can be keys to the healing of our community. We can build a heritage of blessing for generations to come. What an exciting prospect!

Women of color can walk in victory over our past failures, wrongs others have done, and even future traps. We can provide blessings for our children, grandchildren and future generations. I want to impart a vision of the future.

It's time for a new thing. When African American Christian women realize that it's our time and allow God's Spirit to do a cleansing, healing and renewal in our lives, we will begin to operate as the keys we are destined to be. As we operate as keys to change, individuals, families, neighborhoods, cities and this entire country will be affected.

What Can We Expect in This New Thing?

As African American Christian women grow in their love for God and each other, they will learn to share each other's burdens and be transparent with each other. In the new thing, a lot of healing and growing will take place in more intimate settings than large group meetings, retreats and church services afford us. Home fellowships, Sunday school classes and other small groups will become increasingly important in ministry to women.

There is an excitement for some of us when we are in a large group setting. The music, the praise and worship, the motivational messages get us pumped up. But many of us are becoming more and more dissatisfied with the aftermath. The thrill leaves so quickly. There is a place for the large, but there is a valid place for the small setting that allows for relationship building. Though many of us are hiding in the large settings, we really long for the place that will allow us to take our mask off. At the same time, we're scared to let others see what's under our mask. We run from what we want.

As our masks come down and we begin to get our identity from Christ instead of from what others think about us, we will be renewed in our attitudes about ourselves. When we accept God's thoughts toward us, it changes the whole chemistry of our relationship to others. Change will be released to others.

The family of God (the church) can begin to function as one and be the force God intended her to be in this world as African American women come into their places.

Eventually, we will see African American women strong enough to administer forgiveness to those who have been used to hurt, reject and ostracize them. They will begin to extend the same love-covering beyond their own community to others in the body of Christ. African American women can pray that those whose attitudes of racism have bound them in fear and hatred will be released from their error.

Second to None in the Throne Room

In the new thing, we can also expect to see prayer increasing. First, we will learn to pray the prayers of the prayer recipe that are found later in this book. This will facilitate our personal healing. But then our whole understanding of prayer will change. We will begin to approach prayer more from the standpoint of what God wants rather than one of giving God our shopping lists.

Sojourner Truth, Ida B. Wells, Susan B. Anthony, Mary McLeod Bethune, Harriet Tubman, Rosa Parks—all women you may be familiar with—have fought for freedom. In the struggle for liberty and justice for blacks and women, African American women have played a pivotal role. Though battles have been fought and won on many natural fronts, such as voting, riding buses, and access to education, the war for freedom is still in progress.

Denise, Earnestine, Demi, Lynette, Terry, Hivenna, Venessa—women you probably have not heard of—have also fought some battles for freedom. They have fought on their knees for sons, daughters, husbands, ex-husbands, sisters, grandchildren, nephews, fathers, friends, brothers and mothers. Others have fought against the demons of addiction, infidelity, immorality, rebelliousness and sickness in the lives of their loved ones. Many have won victories of marriages staying together, salvation, health and real freedom.

In our fight, many know the real fight is not with people (flesh and blood), but with authorities, powers and rulers of a spiritual nature (Ephesians 6:10). It's time to do battle on a different front. It's time to tell spiritual slave masters "Let our people go!"

God is now calling women, especially African American women to take a key role in a spiritual battle. God can reverse the negative effects of generational curses in our homes, cities and this nation . . . when African American women use the weapon of prayer.

Contrary to much that we have been conditioned to believe, God loves African American women as much as he loves anyone else. He has unique plans for us no one else can carry out.

A woman who learns the proper use of prayer is an instrument of righteousness. In this way she offers her body as a sacrifice unto the Lord. In this way she pours out God's unconditional love upon others.

God is doing a new thing. He has good plans for our future. Much of what God is doing relates to a new understanding of prayer. If African American Christian women prayed like God wants us to pray, the power of God could be unleashed for change in our families, communities, churches and this nation.

I read a book some time ago by Evelyn Christenson, *What Happens when Women Pray.* I was so inspired by the possibility of what prayer could do in our community. We all need to catch a vision of what prayer can do.

Do you get the idea that the subject of prayer is a passion of mine? Well, it is. Did somebody pray for you? Did they have you on their mind? Did they take the time to intercede for you? Well, let me tell you that's exactly what happened to me. I'm alive today because of the prayers of others, probably sane too. (No comments from the peanut gallery.) At the age of seventeen, I had a rare blood disease. I wasn't supposed to make it. But prayer brought me through. Even the doctor said I was a miracle.

So what could happen if African American women prayed? Isaiah 43:20 tells us of God's ability, "I give waters in the wilderness and rivers in the desert, to give drink to My people, My chosen."

Our cities, where most ethnic groups live in America, are certainly desert places. But God wants to give us refreshing water. Our cities can become cities of light! It can happen! God can teach us to labor in prayer until this baby of "change" is delivered to our cities.

What could happen if African American Christian women prayed? If women prayed the way God is calling them to pray, God could send a revival to our land. The revival could prepare the way for a great harvest of souls. As we cry out in prayer for justice, God avenges us of our enemy (Luke 18:3-7). In times of revival we receive back all the enemy has stolen from us and more (Joel 2:19-27).

Prayer is the most powerful force on earth. Effective prayer dwarfs the power of even nuclear energy. Prayer is the main weapon available to anyone in Christ who wants to see change.

Prayer is the first line of attack against those who would like to see us destroyed. It may not be the only key, but it is certainly the key to the first door. Without it, none of the other keys will work. In the hands of God's people, prayer will bring healing to this land!

It is imperative African American Christian women pray. But the kind of prayer that will bring revival to our cities is not normal prayer. God can use African American women and prayer to start revival. He has brought us into his kingdom for such a time as this! Women of color are needed to stand in the gap and pray intercessory prayers.

A Call to Prayer

Exactly what kind of prayer is God calling African American women to at this time? It is prayer similar to labor. We could call it travail. Paul speaks in Galatians 4:19 to "my little children, for whom I travail in birth again until Christ be formed in you." There is a travail necessary to bring birth and one necessary to bring children to maturity.

The prophet Micah in Micah 4:10 says, "Be in pain, and labour to bring forth, O daughter of Zion, like a woman in travail: for now shalt thou go forth out of the city, and thou shalt dwell in the field, and thou shalt go even to Babylon; . . . there the LORD shall redeem thee from the hand of thine enemies" (KJV). Also in Isaiah 66:8, we see that "as soon as Zion travailed, she brought forth her children" (KJV). Zion represents the church.

Is This Really for Women Only?

The Scripture that specifically calls women to prayer is Jeremiah 9:17-21:

> Thus says the LORD of hosts: "Consider and call for the mourning women, that they may come; and send for skillful wailing women,

that they may come. Let them make haste and take up a wailing for us, that our eyes may run down with tears, and our eyelids gush with water. For a voice of wailing is heard from Zion: 'How we are plundered! We are greatly ashamed, because we have forsaken the land, because we have been cast out of our dwellings.' Yet hear the word of the LORD, O women, and let your ear receive the word of his mouth; teach your daughters wailing, and everyone her neighbor a lamentation. For death has come through our windows, has entered our palaces, to kill off the children—no longer to be outside! And the young men—no longer on the streets!"

Go ahead, look up this passage in your own Bible. But women are key here. In this passage we note prayer going beyond making requests. "Let us make haste" indicates an urgency. "A wailing," "tears" and "eyelids gushing out with water" all indicate great intensity. The words uttered, too, are different, as in verse 19: "How are we plundered! We are greatly ashamed, because we have forsaken the land, we have been cast out of our dwellings." The women who are praying are admitting their wrong.

The passage tells us in verse 21 why there is the need for such urgency, intensity and confession. "For death has come through our windows, has entered our palaces, to kill off the children—no longer to be outside! And the young men—no longer on the streets!" Sounds a lot like our urban areas today, doesn't it?

Cocaine, other drugs, alcohol, promiscuous lifestyles, suicide, violence, the New Age movement, cults, gangs, homosexuality and much more are swallowing up our African American youth, our children. Loneliness, hopelessness, despair and debt are doing their damage in black families.

Is death not coming into the windows of many African American families to cut off the children? Have you read in the papers about little girls murdered in their own homes, AIDS capturing more victims, suicide threatening to take away more young lives, abortions taking thousands daily? African American women, we need to respond to this call to prayer now!

Do we need to wait before we take up wailing? When is enough enough? What will it take before we make haste to pray with an intensity that is beyond our normal supplications? These are our sons, nephews, daughters, nieces, granddaughters, grandsons and neighbors. This is the future generation. Perhaps the next Billy Graham is among them. Do we sit idly by and let them be picked off one by one?

The call is going out now to mourning women and wise (cunning) women to take up a wailing that our children might be spared. The call is going out to African American Christian women who are willing to pray with an intensity beyond the norm, willing to leave the familiar and traditional behind. Desperate circumstances call for drastic measures, maybe even some emotional involvement!

Prayer is a large part of the ministry in the home. As African American Christian mothers seek God in prayer, they will train their children by the wisdom God gives. Through prayer, women, aunts, grandmothers, teachers will take authority over a spiritual enemy as he tries to bring his wares into the life of the children in their lives. As African American Christian women stay close to God, many will be warned of the plans of evil before they come to pass.

African American Christian women need to pray children away from the plans and traps of the evil one and into God's hands for God's use and glory. Women are keepers and women are also keys. Yes, at this time, this critical time, prayer—the key to the front door—is needed.

African American women can begin to come together in corporate settings to pray for issues in our cities. They can also join together to pray and fast for relatives' lives that are still under bondage. Together they can pray and strategize to release others from spiritual prisons.

Christians even from different denominations can come together, refusing to let those differences deter them from the work of prayer. Though they may still believe differently or even have different ways of praying, they will avoid offending each other and agree to work for that which is most important change in our homes and communities.

Praying and teaching are not the only reason to come together. Many of the gatherings can turn into times of singing and testimonies of victory. More time will probably be spent in praising God than in making request as the "new thing" continues. As God's blessings begin to flow in abundance, more time will of necessity be taken to praise God for his goodness.

In this chapter we have examined the tremendous spiritual potential and prayer power of African American Christian women. But there are also some real dangers.

Danger for Women

Hebrews 12:15 says to be careful not to let bitterness root into your soul "lest . . . many become defiled." It is crucial that the woman of God learn how to see through and rise above the plan of defeat. Unfortunately, whether in her home or with others, a woman's service can be easily tainted. It is possible that the Holy Spirit may not be able to flow through her in a pure way. Without a transforming work of God's Spirit, she may do more harm than good in the kingdom of God.

This danger stems from bitterness allowed to root into the spirit because of past offenses. The symptoms include an unforgiving spirit, relationship problems, backbiting, rebellious attitudes, being extremely opinionated, a reluctance to trust God and a "chip on the shoulder" about God, men, people in authority and other races.

Karen encountered many hardships as a child. Her father constantly abused her mother. Her mother responded by committing adultery repeatedly. Karen lied to her friends when they asked about the different men who came to pick her mom up in the evenings after her father left for his night job: "Oh, that's just my cousin from out of town." Karen internalized her embarrassment, anger and pain during her growing up years.

She went to college in another state right after high school to get away from all the conflict in her house. When she returned her mother had divorced her father and moved a boyfriend into their house.

Karen became a Christian shortly after finishing college. Extremely gifted in the area of teaching, she committed herself to the adult class at her church. A few years later she married. Karen violently argued with her husband anytime he glanced at another woman. Her hurts from the past caused severe jealousy and mistrust with her new husband. Eventually, the marriage failed and her husband remarried. Karen grew increasingly bitter. She never confided in anyone about her feelings and continued to faithfully attend church and teach the adult class. Her bitter spirit spilled over into her teaching. Instead of women coming to forgive and love unconditionally, the women in her class picked up her bitter attitude.

Karen's story is typical of several women who are active in our churches today. Outwardly they present a strong appearance but inwardly they are hurting and the wounds have turned to bitterness. The bitter woman will be useless in helping other women overcome evil. Error may begin to enter her message.

Without hearing from God about her worth, a woman will operate out of a sense of inferiority, or will continue to struggle to prove she is just as capable. The woman who has not fully allowed God to heal her will tend to fear other people's opinions, seeking their approval instead of God's. She will often turn back when persecuted or when things are not working out just like she thought God would do it.

The consequences: little confidence in prayer or misuse of prayer to manipulate and change people. This woman may be a great communicator, but will have no prayer power. She won't be able to get a prayer through.

In my opinion, we have enough gifted communicators—teachers, preachers, speakers and the like, but give me a few females who like Elijah have an audience with God and can call down fire from heaven and we might see some change in the African American community.

Yes, God has great plans for African American women as second to none in the throne room. I am excited about what God has in store for us.

Questions for Thought and Action

1. There's a list of problems in the chapter: relationship, financial, health, time management, boss, loneliness, weight, clutter control, work, children, car. Which of these do you relate to? Add others if desired.

2. What are some of the things from books in the New Testament that we are told to do with/for one another that are only possible in a small group setting?

3. Joel 2:19-27 tells us of being given back what has been taken from us. Read Luke 18:1-8 and relate how prayer is vital to that process.

4. Read Jeremiah 9:17-21, especially verse 21. Give some examples of things you've read in the newspaper or have heard on the news in the last few months that attests to death taking our young.

5. What experience have you had with the power of prayer?

6. *Going deeper:* What does Scripture tells us of Elijah's prayer power (James 5:17-18)? What could happen to your family (neighborhood or church) if three people with the prayer power Elijah exhibited would join together?

7. If you have detected a "bitterness" problem in your life or in the life of someone you care about, what are some of the steps you can take to get rid of it?

8. Take a moment now to meditate upon and pray aloud this prayer. (If you cannot pray it at this time, perhaps you will be able to at a later time.) "Father, teach me to persist in prayer for the things you want to do in my life and in the lives of my family, fellow church members, coworkers or neighbors. Give me your burdens. Give me others who will join me. I make myself available to you even for you to give me tears so that the death that is taking away our children would cease."

3

woundeo hearts—
our biggest problem

• •

*The LORD is near to those who have a broken heart,
and saves such as have a contrite spirit. (PSALM 34:18)*

Well, so far either you are excited about how God wants to use you as an African American women or you may be totally frustrated and thinking *That's really nice, but I just don't see it. Do you know my mama, my grandmother? Do you know the men in my family? Do you know me?!! . . . I don't think so.*

I remember being invited to speak for a women's conference a few years ago. Most of the time arrangements are made for me to stay in a hotel, but this time I was asked if I would mind staying with one of the ladies involved. I agreed to the request, not knowing that God had something in store for me. The evening after the conference before going to bed, my gracious hostess had some things to share with me.

This dear lady shared with me how her husband was in prison for molesting their daughter. She was now for all intents and purposes a single parent trying to raise her children and coping with all she had endured. After hearing her story, I literally cried myself to sleep. I was so grieved over the heartbreak of this beautiful Christian lady. I believe God let me in on the grief in his heart that he has for African American women and the pain we endure.

Sometimes I look at the lives of African American women and just wonder how we "got over" and how we are getting over now. Many of us go through so much, have gone through so much, it is heart-rending to hear the stories. My heart aches for the pain many of my sisters go through. Sometimes I do not know what to say. At times I have even questioned God about the Scripture that says he does not put any more on us than we can bear (1 Corinthians 10:13).

It's like "God, I know what your Word says, but this one looks like it might be an exception. What's up with this?" After hearing this lady's story and eventually hearing about the daughter's own marital problems, I am more and more convinced that a calculated plan has been put into operation to make African American women beat-down, hopeless and ineffective. This plan has been designed to make African American women feel inferior and beyond God's use.

Christian women of color have been forced into fighting so many other battles, it's no wonder we don't have the time or energy to enlist in God's army and fight battles for him. When it takes all you can muster up just to get the kids to the dozen places they need to go, pay the bills, argue over child support, see about the sibling in prison, wonder whether the lights or the phone will get turned off first, make an appointment with the teacher because your child hasn't been doing his work, and then your boss starts to act up, talking about how your production is not up to par—please! You might go postal and you don't even work in a post office, let alone have the time to visit one!

As a result of the wounds we suffer, a sizable portion of the army designed to be on God's side is not fighting the real enemy. African American women could win many battles if we just realize God can use the tactics of the enemy for his own purposes as he prepares his army to reap a harvest.

Trained warriors are needed to go into enemy territory to release prisoners. Think of it as "boot camp." Many African American women are in this boot camp, but have not understood how God could use the special difficulties they face.

As I see the pain and complaining of African American women, it has become clear to me that not understanding God's purposes only prolongs the anguish. It is my hope that insight will help women use their painful experiences to properly direct their anger and use their energy to rescue those caught up in spiritual prisons.

Knowing the immense influence that godly African American women can have on this country, someone has launched a vicious attack against them. The one behind this calculated plan has tried to stop everything God originally designed. The purpose of this attack is to prevent us from knowing God's love and walking in God's purposes. When we don't know the love of our Father God, we run from rather than to him. Of course, we can't fulfill our God-ordained purpose when we live afar from God.

As I have already mentioned, I am more convinced than ever that God wants to use African American women as keys to change.

I am also more convinced than I have ever been of the extreme difficulty of that ever happening. As I interact with others and understand from their experiences what we have to cope with on a daily basis, I'm aware that what I believe God desires to do in African American women is next to an impossibility. I'm even more convinced because God has shown me how easy it is for me to fall into traps, getting sidetracked from his purposes.

It's Even Worse for Us
Sisters of color, it's you who have had the hardest fight to stay out of the bondage to fear, low self-esteem, bitterness and unforgiveness. The African American female must literally fight to keep from drowning under the negative feelings of rejection and inferiority.

Our hair has never been quite good enough. Our skin color or gender has kept us out of jobs or promotions and away from better grades. Our education was thought to be inferior.

Not only men have offended us, but racial prejudice has been an offense. We have had many wounds inflicted on us. We've carried the scars of rejection all of our life. Some of us were not wanted. Many of us have been emotionally, physically and sexually abused. Wounds, rejection, and abuse all play into the plan of keeping us from our purposes.

Sometimes the men we married find it hard or nearly impossible to get it together. Sometimes they haven't been able to provide for us. Some men have not even bothered to marry us. They make babies and leave us to care for them. Many of them take their anger at society out on us.

Some of our sons and daughters don't do well in school. Others are always getting into trouble. We did the best we knew how in raising them, yet some are in jail, some on drugs, some walking the streets, some living on the street, some in gangs, some not taking care of their families, some with AIDS. That was not how we brought them up.

Yes, we live with fear, guilt and condemnation. We harbor deep hurts and resentments. We have so much to be bitter about and it is eating at us inside. These things drive us to alcohol, drugs, sex, food, and even to church. But we don't find lasting relief, because not even church can give the relief Jesus gives.

A good number of African American professional women have learned to pull themselves up in spite of everything. They've got their degrees, some their Ph.D.s. They have the big houses, luxury cars, prestigious jobs and the whole bit. They have proven they can make it. But not even success can ease the inner pain.

African American women who have unhealthy relationships have bought the myth of the independent black woman who does not need any man. "It's time to get back at them. Use *them* now. We'll be a success whether they care to come along or not. They've held us back too long. If they are too insecure, stoned, strung out on drugs, womanizing and fearful, we'll do it by ourselves—without them."

Inside the shells of material or career success is a hurting, lonely little black girl. This girl may have compromised her conscience. This is the girl Jesus loves, accepts and forgives, but she does not really feel acceptable. Her only hope is God.

Jesus does not hold anything against us. Nothing grieves him more than our indifference to him. He's paid for our wrong, and he does not want us to continue to give ground to evil. He's even made his life available to us so we would not have to continue in our negative patterns of behavior. He's hurt when we don't accept what he has made available for us.

The plan against us has worked. African American women have had a terrible weight of lies placed within our souls. We get confirmations of our inferiority from everywhere. The "proof" is hard to ignore.

Not only do we have insurmountable daily struggles, African American Christian women have issues, many issues. We have attitude issues. We have issues with submission and authority. We have problems with our tongues. We have roots of bitterness. We have anger issues. We have control issues. We have idolatry issues. That's just a beginning.

But what it all boils down to is that to fulfill the vision we discussed in the last chapter of being women of prayer will take an act of God. Well, I happen to believe God is putting on a class act right now. He told us about what he was going to do in the last days in Joel. "And it shall come to pass afterward that I will pour out My Spirit on all flesh; your sons and your daughters shall prophesy, your old men shall dream dreams, your young men shall see visions. And also on My menservants and on My maidservants I will pour out My Spirit in those days" (Joel 2:28-29).

That's an act of God. God is more than able to do it. In fact, he does not mind giving himself a distinct disadvantage as he proves himself to be the Almighty God that he is, just like when he weeded down Gideon's army so that everyone would know it was God who got the victory (Judges 7).

I also believe that in the days we're living in, God is preparing an army of overcomers who by their obedience to him will be participants with him as he wraps up things on planet earth. It is imperative that *all* members of God's family, no matter what ethnic background, gender or national heritage, be made ready to work together in the oneness needed for a victorious army.

From the specific emphasis in Joel of women being part of this move of God, it is obvious that women will have an important place in this army. I'm saying that women of color have a major place as members in God's army in these days that we're living in.

The calculated plan to keep African American women AWOL (absent without leave) actually started in the Garden of Eden. But for us, it had a second major help with the experience of slavery in this country. We will discuss the attack on women and the attack on African Americans later on in separate chapters. But here we will see how the double whammy on African American women has caused a very serious problem.

Yes, we have problems; we have issues. We've been wounded. Yes, we're messed up. Who wouldn't be if they have endured what many of us have endured? It's the grace of God that more of us are not insane. I marveled that the lady I mentioned in the beginning of this chapter still loves and serves the Lord. In fact, she started a support group for women and children who have gone through similar hurt.

Let me make it clear: the one who is behind the calculated plan to keep us useless in God's army has set a destructive course for society's treatment of women and double rejection of African American women. This whole thing is a set up from the beginning of time. The devastating result of the calculated plan against you and me is wounded or broken hearts. With a wounded heart, a woman will build walls around herself as a protection from more pain and rejection.

Unfortunately these walls keep her away from Jesus, the true lover of her soul, others who can help her see the Father's love and even her own self. As a result many African American women are shells of the full person they have a potential of being. Many are lonely and isolated, with tremendous problems relating to others.

Many African American women suffer from wounded hearts. A woman with a wounded heart will have a hidden rift with God and may believe he is responsible for her pain. Women with wounded hearts do not know how to live out the purposes of God.

Women who have been wounded are often out of control. They have problems with explosive anger or depression, with appetites for food, drugs or excitement. Others tend to be perfectionists and make acceptance conditional upon performance.

If a woman has had a poor relationship with her father or any authority figure, she will have a hard time trusting and maintaining a good relationship with her heavenly Father. She will often believe that God is unfair, doubt he has her best interests at heart, and give her mind to him but not her affection. Consequently she will never reach her full potential in God.

This is true even for women who are thought to be, or think of themselves as good Christians.

A Wounded Heart Hidden Inside African American Women

Many of the wounds of African American women are due to an attack on her sexuality. My friend Victoria Johnson wrote *Restoring Broken Vessels: Confronting the Attack on Female Sexuality* in 1995. This book has given insight to many women. As Victoria speaks to women around the country, many confide in her that they have been raped, molested or wounded sexually in some way. Many times they tell her that they have never told anyone this information. Yet, after years, they are still in bondage. Unfortunately this takes place among the church community, deacons and pastors much more than we'd like to admit.

The magnitude of the problem at times seems overwhelming. But fortunately God is able to bring healing to the deepest wounds. Though it appears the plan has been successful in keeping women from God's best, that will not continue as women realize they have choices to abandon the set-up by going all the way over to God's side.

Many women turn to religious form and structure. Unfortunately many of these religious women have a form of godliness, but their very lives deny the power of God (2 Timothy 3:5).

In *Movin' On Up: A Woman's Guide Beyond Religion to Spirit Liv-*

ing I define religion as talk and activity. In that book I take a look at my own history of being involved in a lot of religious activity, but not reality. We're good at that, but how much of it is the power of God?

A quote from *Movin' On Up:*

> A friend of mine told me about the night she spoke at one of the largest (African American) churches in this country. She spoke on the hurting woman. An altar call was given after she spoke, and the tremendous response of the women to the altar call amazed everyone. The pastor of the church could not believe the number of hurting women in his church.

Our churches are filled with wounded, out of control women who are not rooted in their God-ordained purpose. Churches are good places for the wounded to hide out. In the years I've been in ministry to women, I've had ample time to look under your and my masks. It *don't* look very pretty under *dare*. God Almighty is willing to work on us. Are we willing to allow him to do it?

Unfortunately African American women contribute to the destructive cycle: we receive abuse, experience the pain of rejection, then react negatively toward others. We have also lost love and respect for African American men. Some of our African American men as well as men from other ethnic groups, have been the instruments of our pain. Since many men, especially husbands and fathers, are in positions of authority in our lives, respect in God's eyes is very important (Ephesians 5:33; Exodus 20:12). The lack of respect that we have for authority carries over to God.

It's not a secret that a lot of strife, tension and confusion exist in the relationships between black men and women. The wedge already existing between males and females is magnified when men and women have both experienced hurt and rejection and do not know their spiritual destiny. As children sense even nonverbal strife and contention between men and women, it has a powerfully negative effect on them, an effect that is made worse by discipline done out of anger.

Children need our blessing but are cursed from the lips of parents.

We have participated too often in passing on to our children the very same curses that have been put on our race by others.

Do these phrases sound familiar? Chances are, you've heard them before. Hopefully you've never used them:

"You're never going to amount to anything."

"Boy, you're just like your daddy, the good for nothing low-down dog."

"Girl, with your fast self, you're going to get pregnant just like your aunt Bessie."

"I don't know what's wrong with you. You must be out of your mind."

Children of any color vitally need acceptance, kindness, encouragement, affection and instruction, among other things. Women with broken hearts who are trying to make marital relationships work do not always have the strength to give nurture, encouragement and protection to their children.

It has been possible to destroy whole generations because of attacks against women.

Disheartened women. Broken families. Troubled communities. Cities that need healing. People, our entire nation needs healing.

There Is Hope . . .
There is one antidote to all that has been planned against us. There is one truth that when applied will erase all that has been done over years. The truth is: God loves, values and has a purpose for us. That truth came through Jesus.

If we could only get a true knowledge and understanding of God's love and care! If we as women could really experience that love for all it really is, the results would be dynamic! If that love could get beyond our intellectual knowledge and really sink into our being, we would not need to fear, feel insecure or be bitter toward anyone.

How can we experience that love? We will need to be awakened to truth. God will need to move among us and show us that love. To those who are willing, God can reveal more and more of his sweet presence to us.

God has the power to break through what has happened from the beginning of time until now. He can do a new thing in us to refute all of the lies we have believed. He can correct and bring back to original order what has taken thousands of years to distort.

As long as African American women continue to fall into the traps that have been set for us, we will continue to carry out the wrong plan upon the earth. But if we can look behind the smoke screen to see exactly what is happening, we could learn to walk a different way. We could begin to cooperate with God's plan. We could become tools in God's hands.

Haven't you heard the good news? We've been set free by the blood of the Lamb. The emancipation proclamation has already been signed; the one who benefited from our bondage just didn't want us to know. Now, we'll have to go through deprogramming to get all of those false ideas and attitudes out of our system. We need to wipe everything out of our emotions and start over with a clean slate.

Women of color especially need to put a lot of our religious training on the line. Ironically, the Bible is often misquoted or passages are taken out of context. All of us need to search the Scriptures for ourselves to see if what our teachers are saying is true. I expect you to do the same concerning the things I'm saying in this book. God will help you sort the truth from error.

African American women, it's time we put our spiritual armor on and fight the real war (Ephesians 6:10-17). It's time we took up our spiritual weapons and win a few battles. It's time we put ourselves under God's authority. It's time we become weapons in the hand of God. It's time we demonstrate the victory secured at the cross (Colossians 2:15).

Our Responsibility

There is plenty of blame to go around. All believers at some time have made wrong choices, not obeyed God's Word and been ignorant of truth. Often we have not known how to get out of the destructive cycles. The plan against us has succeeded to a large degree because we have cooperated.

With truth, African American women are responsible to put a stop to all that has been done in our homes and communities. If we choose to let it continue, we will only have ourselves to blame.

I have been truly inspired by Harriet Tubman's story. Upon realizing the wrong done against her people, she dedicated her life to bringing them to freedom. She was a woman of God. We need God, and God needs a few female Moseses like Harriet to be able to make a dent in the spiritual slavery many of us are under.

Though we will spend time in this book talking about what has been done to us by others, by no means do we want to infer that black women have no responsibility for themselves and those whom God puts in their lives.

We have played our part in falling into and staying in the traps set up for us. We have played a part in keeping others in spiritual prisons.

It's not that we have done anything out of the ordinary. Our responses have been natural responses. But Christians are without excuse. We have the resources to respond above the natural.

We must turn from these ways. As we realize how we have been tricked and broken by someone very sinister, we can ask God to put our heart back together.

Things We Have to Settle

We will have to take responsibility for our wrongs. We will have to admit them. We cannot cover our own sin (Proverbs 28:13). We will have to take responsibility for our part before we can expect God to come to our defense.

We will have to forgive. When we forgive, God gives us the power to go even further. He can help us bring life to those who have offended us.

We've actually blocked God's love, acceptance and forgiveness from getting through to others by our attitudes and behavior. We may be the only Jesus some will ever see. What kind of Jesus do we portray—an angry, bitter, proud Jesus? That's a false image. That's not Jesus. That's our flesh. Jesus is meek, lowly, humble. He knows how to be angry, but he does not sin. He does not hold it.

There is good news! God promises to heal the broken in heart (Psalm 147:3). God says he is near the brokenhearted (Psalm 34:18). There is tremendous hope for African American women. Let us fall on our faces before God and get our wounded hearts bound up and receive a touch of new life. We can then be used of God to bring healing to others.

God is putting many of our lives back together again. Many of us are going through tremendous pain and struggles in our lives because God is doing open-heart surgery on us. He is melting the bitterness. We have to submit no matter how painful it is. The pain does not last forever. We may need to shed tears. It is part of the healing process.

We do not want our heart condition to get worse. We must not let the pain force us off the operating table in the middle of open-heart surgery. We must settle in our hearts we will go through the healing process.

African American women have a special place in God's purposes. African American women can be chosen vessels, keys to change. There is a vicious plan against us. As others have abused us, we suffer brokenness in the seat of our emotions and affections. That has caused us to be cold-hearted and hardhearted.

African American women have difficulty trusting authority, nurturing children and carrying out God's purposes of training, influencing and cooperating with others.

It's time this whole cycle stopped. African American women can put a stop to it. But we can only stop it if we are willing to live in the realm of the Spirit. It is in this realm we can regain our original purpose and be an instrument in God's hand.

All hurts of the past must be laid on Jesus Christ. It is in the healing process that a woman comes to the understanding of God's love and unique purposes. Once a woman has undergone the healing process successfully, she will be free to be all that God wants her to be in his army. "In all your getting, get understanding" (Proverbs 4:7). Sisters, we've got to continue to understand God's plans for us.

Questions for Thought and Action

1. Read Psalm 34:18, noting the surrounding text. Read it in at least one other version or translation such as NIV, NLT, Amplified or NAS. Who wrote the passage? Who are the brokenhearted? What does that tell you about how God wants to help us?

2. Read Exodus 3:7-9. Think about the possibility that God has seen your pain and struggle and that he wants to do something about it. How does that makes you feel?

3. Have you ever felt you may be an exception to the Scripture found in 1 Corinthians 10:13 that says God does not allow us to be tempted beyond what we are able? Explain why or why not.

4. *Going deeper:* When I was growing up, just looking at television was proof I wasn't good enough. What "proofs" have been a part of your life? Find Scripture that counters that "proof." You might want to use a promise book or talk to other Christians as you look.

5. Why would a calculated attack against women eventually affect whole communities?

What are some of the things we as African American women can do to begin to see change?

6. The truth is God loves, values and has a purpose for _____. That truth came through Jesus. Write the above statement with your name inserted in the last blank and say it aloud several times. If you are in a group, you might say or pray it for one another.

7. Take a moment now to meditate upon and pray aloud this prayer. (If you cannot pray it at this time, perhaps you will be able to at a later time.) "Father, please give me fresh insight and understanding of your love for me. I desire every hindrance to knowing, believing and understanding your love for me to be removed. I desire to be rid of all false idols and attitudes. Do a miraculous work in my heart and mind by making me to know the truth of your love for me."

part 2

understanding
the enemy's plan

4

the plan against african americans

See to it that no one misses the grace of God and that no bitter root grows up to cause trouble and defile many. (HEBREWS 12:15 NIV)

I'm tired of the black community always being put in a negative light," complained a caller to the host of a local Christian radio talk show. The host had stated that abortions were more prevalent in the African American community than in non-minority communities. The caller challenged him by referring to statistics that refuted the host's claim.

One of the questions African Americans often struggle with is whether God loves them less than others. To many it appears the blessings of God are upon other races, but his curse is on us. Why is it that African Americans seem to suffer more? If God has loved us the same as everyone else, why does it seem he has not come though for us?

Is there a curse on the African American community? Yes, but not the kind of curse we have historically heard about. God is not the author of this curse. I guess this is a good a place as any to reveal to you who the sinister author of the plan against African American women is. He's the one we've been alluding to for the last few chapters who has it in for African American women, who is their enemy. I'll mention who he is right now, and in another chapter we'll expose him further.

Remember Flip Wilson and his saying "The devil made me do it"? Well, the enemy of African American women is the devil. Yes, the devil is the one behind the wounds African American women suffer. He's the one who made sure you were messed up so that he could be sure your offspring were messed up and on and on it goes.

This chapter will delve into the role that slavery had on African American females. We're not going into the past, drudging up things so that we can get bitter. No, that's probably already happened. My purpose in going to the root of some of our issues is to dig them up, the roots, that is.

As a subculture in the United States, some real differences exist between our community and other communities. We do seem to suffer disproportionately. Relatively more of our people have AIDS. More are in prisons, hospitals, mental institutions, unemployment lines, poverty and broken homes. These are known facts.

Are black women at the low end of the totem pole? Neither financial or health statistics look good.

According to the Bureau of the Census for 2000, the median income for black females was at the bottom. According to the Bureau of Labor Statistics in 2000, unemployment rates were twice as high for black women as for white women and white men. Only unemployment rates for black men were higher than black women.

The National Women's Health Information Center indicates suicide rates are rising among black females. They also report a rise in depression symptoms for black teenage females compared to white teenage females. The Cancer Institute reports the mortality rate from breast cancer increased for black females while it decreased for white females in the same period (1973 to 1995). In 2001 the Center for Disease Control reports out of all new HIV/AIDS cases among all women in the United States, black women make up two-thirds.

We should be tired of the enemy having such open inroads into our community and among our people. It is time for African Americans who know God to wake up and shut the doors of our communities to evil.

It is the devil who has sought to make African Americans feel inferior, less important, less loved by God, worthless and nearly useless in the kingdom of God. Satan has used everything at his disposal, including "Christians" and out-of-context Scripture to do his dirty work.

Slavery: Forming a Bitter Root

Most of Satan's schemes against African Americans are rooted in the experience of slavery. Much of the anger in our communities has come from a root of bitterness beginning during slavery and passed down from generation to generation.

You know the history. In slavery we as a people were severely wronged. Our women were raped. Our families were separated. As a people, we were used and abused. Out of the frustration and helplessness our ancestors experienced, bitterness no doubt found root in their souls.

This bitterness has been passed from parents to children because of few other places to vent frustration. When people are wronged by those who are over them, they will often take it out on the people who are under their control. Our disturbing tendency to discipline our children out of anger originated in slavery. This is experienced as rejection by children.

This angry discipline has continued through the centuries. Even after slavery was over, parents still had to deal with much rejection and frustration from society. In matters of discipline they often reverted back to the example of their parents.

The inability to put together in their minds and emotions the treatment of their parents often causes African American children to suffer from broken hearts. They know in their minds their parents love them, but have a hard time dealing with parental anger. This has in turn led to parental disrespect.

Children in African American communities grow up with a lot of pain. Comfort and affection could have healed some of the pain, but parents, frustrated and just trying to survive in a hostile world, have little energy for affection. Add the wedge placed between men and women in our communities, and you have a situation in which it is very difficult for many to have a healthy childhood. You know, that includes you too. A lot of us grew up too soon.

Listen to this account from an African American woman who just recently became a single parent:

> When I come home from work, I barely have enough energy to make it through the door. It's not that my job is so hard, but it's not the kind of work I want to do . . . and the people at work, Lord have mercy, they have issues. Just to get through the day without telling someone off or getting told off myself is a miracle. By the time I get home and the kids want me to listen to their school stories and help them with homework, I'm wiped out. All I can think about is getting into that bed and sleeping the night away. Or popping in a good movie and imagining I'm one of the characters who has a life with a happy ending. I know my children sense my "get away from me, I'm tired, I don't want to deal with you" attitude. I want to love them and be affectionate. I know they need it, especially since their father and I have split up and he's out of the picture. But I just don't seem to have the heart or the energy.

The Consequences Spread Through the Black Community

A lot of what goes on in our community was rooted in slavery. Since families were broken at the will of the slave masters, the family relationship was sabotaged. It was too painful for a man to really care for a woman and then be sold somewhere else. Women became objects to fulfill sexual desires. This lack of respect has been passed down through the generations.

We must also consider the problems we have respecting authority.

Again, look at the pattern established in slavery. How much respect can a normal human being have for someone who treats him as an animal?

This plan has reached deep into our communities to cause pain, discord and every kind of evil. This has been the evil one's ultimate aim. His schemes are well orchestrated to continue a cycle of destruction from generation to generation.

How Slavery Still Affects Us

Francis Frangipane illustrates in this excerpt from an article appearing in the *Spirit of God's Kingdom* newsletter, June 1991:

> Although slavery was legally abolished in the eighteen-hundreds, racism continued. Its wounds remain today in the souls of many blacks, propelling a growing percentage of young black men toward violence.
>
> These men neither understand their actions nor can they find a way out of the shroud of death which broods over their neighborhoods.
>
> The fact is, much of the violence in our cities today is the bitter fruit of a tree the white race cultivated in the soil of racism and slavery.
>
> In America today one in four black males over twenty-one is in some form of incarceration. And the highest cause of death among black men under twenty-five is homicide. It is only by the grace of God, who became the strength of the black man early in his struggle, that the remaining majority found creative and productive ways to apply their lives.

Not long ago I was in the car with my fifteen-year-old son, Nosa, as he was beginning to learn to drive. I think a police car passed us, and I became overwhelmed with the thought that as a young black male driving, he probably would be pulled over by police just because he was black. A sense of sadness came over me.

I'm sure many of us notice how the store clerks will watch young black men with the eye of a hawk. It's got to be unnerving. I feel for my sons. Worrying about our children's safety in our schools, in this society that is stacked against them, can give you ulcers.

Having to work ten times harder just to get a promotion or keep a job will raise your blood pressure. It's stressful to always feel like you're guilty until proven innocent. Is it any wonder our health is affected? Add to that the way we harm our own bodies with alcohol, drugs and food. Our health suffers disproportionately. Also our bodies were not designed to house bitterness and anger. The evil one knows that. His plan is working.

We are an embittered people. Becoming a Christian does not necessarily take the anger away. In fact, it presents a new set of questions.

Roots of Deception in American Christianity

We often wonder why it appears God's favor on this land may be running out. Why is judgment allowed in a country God has seemed to bless for so long? The way African Americans were and still are treated in this country is certainly one of the reasons. When people are hearers of the Word and not doers, they deceive themselves (James 1:22).

Christianity in America is under a serious web of deception rooted in the experience of slavery in this country. It is important to see how the sins of our spiritual fathers still affect us today. It is important to look at history to understand what we have inherited. We need to know what we are dealing with. We need to know how we today can reverse the curse of what others have brought into our lives.

The following quote, again from Francis Frangipane, cuts to the root of the problem. It comes from the newsletter cited earlier:

The Lord set a standard and put it in the spirit of America. Our founding fathers believed, and were willing to die for the truth, "that all men were created equal." They understood that every individual was "endowed by their creator with certain inalienable rights-life, liberty, and the pursuit of happiness." God has taken our own words and is using them to judge us. For we fought a war to secure freedom and then denied it to the blacks.

Racial prejudice among the people who are not of God is one thing, but the same spirit among those who claim to be of God is something entirely different. How is it that people can say they love God yet hate their African American brothers and sisters that they brought here as slaves and introduced to the God of Abraham, Isaac and Jacob?

In *The Arrogance of Faith,* author Forrest G. Wood documents the role "Christians" had in bringing slaves to America, justifying slavery and the ill treatment of slaves and defending the "rights" of Americans to keep slavery going even when God began to raise up true ministers who began to challenge those ideas. It is tragic that this is in the history of American Christianity.

Wood says racism within the Christian ranks completely compromised and "subverted" the principles upon which this country has stood, principles that emphasized peace and good will. He makes the point that believers often refused to recognize the error of racism.

Eleven o'clock Sunday mornings is said to be the most segregated hour of the week. Racial barriers are so rooted in the American culture, many do not know to what extent it is present within them. Few have any idea of how much the Lord Jesus Christ hates it and is offended by it.

I believe this is one of the greatest hindrances to God's presence among his own people. Judging by outward appearances is not tolerated in God's kingdom. It is in such direct opposition to his kingdom's principles that it will have to be rooted out of Christians in America before God's presence and favor will rest upon this nation in greater measure.

Racial prejudice is not just a problem others have. Many African American women have deep-seated problems with those from other races. Even if we feel that we have escaped or have sufficiently dealt with the problem of judging others by outward appearances, it would not hurt to just ask God to search us anyway. There might be something hidden back in a remote closet that we haven't been in for years. And if we do not find anything, we still can be tools in God's hand to pray for others who still remain bound by these chains.

Much of the bias against African Americans is not conscious or overt. Unfortunately the ingrained cultural tendencies have not been challenged enough by religious leaders. It is costly, inconvenient and uncomfortable to make changes to accommodate those who are different. The world's system of operating advocates exploitation and continued oppression of the disadvantaged.

Racial prejudice has done a tremendous amount of damage in this country. It is a terrible offense to God. It has literally torn up his family.

Results of Racism in the Body of Christ
The enemy has lies for every group. The four main lies to African American are as follows:
◆ God loves other races more than he loves us.
◆ A curse is on us strictly because of the color of our skin.
◆ We are inferior to others because of the color of our skin.
◆ Even God cannot use us.

Ingrained racial prejudice among the people of God has served to give "proof" to these lies.

As a result of our experiences rooted in slavery, unfortunately many African Americans are put out of commission from God's army because of fear, insecurities, hatred, bitterness, unforgiveness and resentments. The result: devastating loss in the kingdom of God.

The enemy has been very successful in causing destruction in major cities. Many Christians living in these cities are not combating the real enemy. They don't even know who the real redeemer is. Have you ever wondered how there can be a church on almost every corner, and our cities still are in the mess they are in? If we are supposed to be the light, why are our cities so dark?

The vicious cycle against African Americans has been in operation for decades. The barriers that remain among those who claim the name of Jesus are a disgrace to his name. Yet the cycle continues.

Partiality. Prejudice. Hatred. Bitterness. Unforgiveness. We in America will have to face up to these serious issues if we desire God to heal our nation. Though some of these things are changing, it is not enough.

Yes, African Americans may be very religious, but we have a hidden rift with God. We are angry at God. We wonder how and why he let such injustice happen, especially since much of the evil was done in the name of God, under the cloak of "Christianity."

How is it that American Christianity could tolerate such inconsistencies for so long and still refuse to look upon racism as God looks upon it? How could the Bible be used to justify slavery and the inferiority of blacks? Why did God allow us to be slaves? Why didn't God bring us out of slavery sooner? Why is it that when blacks became brothers and sisters in the Lord they were never treated as true brothers and sisters? How is it those same attitudes are prevalent today?

No, we may not necessarily ask these questions out loud. We may not even be aware that these conflicts are in our hearts. But they are there and few have found peace with the nagging questions of *why* and *how.*

But we read the Bible. We see what God says about how we should treat each other as members of the same family. We're not dumb. We know how we've been treated and how we still are not fully accepted. We look at the Bible. We look at reality. We look at the Bible. We look at reality.

Some of the common pat answers of "American Christianity" may appease our minds for a while, but they have never satisfied our hearts. It is time we ask the hard questions, get our answers from God, settle things with him and get on with becoming all he wants us to be. It will take a change in our attitudes, words and actions.

We may be religious as a people, but I think that when we neglect to confront our painful history in this "Christian" nation, we will often have a hidden conflict with the God who "allowed" this. While giving lip service to him, we often end up worshiping other gods. We try very hard to just concentrate on the God of the Bible, but his children, those who are supposed to be our brothers and sisters keep us messed up. No doubt, things are better now than years ago, but it still seems they treat us as tokens and don't really value our worth.

Consequently we have turned to the government as our provider. We have turned to food, alcohol, sex, shopping, drugs, status, and even church for comfort. We have turned to sports, recreation and music to get worth. We turn to relationships to feel secure. We have turned to all these idols instead of turning to God alone. This leads to curses and not the blessings of God.

But there is room for much hope. God often does his greatest work in, among and through those who have been offended the most. Again, light shines best in the deepest darkness. The darkness of sin and wrong against us as a people will give opportunity for God's light to shine upon us in a bright way. Where sin abounds, grace abounds the more. In essence, our experience here can be as redemptive as Joseph's experience was for his family.

How African Americans Are Affected Today

Yes, there is a conspiracy against African Americans. It has been cooked in hell. White American Christians have been used as pawns in the hand of the enemy to carry it out and even continue its effects until this day.

The evil one is using many to carry out his purposes of destroying our community. Along with the institutional church, the government also has played its part in the conspiracy. The government will lie to us about what is safe. To point to just one example, it will not tell our communities that the only spiritually, emotionally and physically safe sex is abstinence until marriage. Even if it did, it does not have the power to help our young men and women maintain abstinence.

The bureaucracy of government has enough problems worrying about how to get more money. It doesn't care how many of us die. The more who die, the better. It doesn't care if we destroy our young through abortions or if we destroy ourselves through drugs. It tells us to just say "no" to drugs, not to whom we should say "yes."

Jesus took upon himself the curse of sin. When individuals continue in sin, they are subject to the judgment of God. But right now, we will consider how people in the Christian community too often judge with improper judgment and curse each other with damaging words.

Christians in America justified slavery and mistreatment of African Americans. But we have not mentioned that white Americans, including those who claimed to be Christians, also cursed African Americans with their mouths. From pulpits it was taught that blacks were less than humans. In books written by "Christians" it was proclaimed that blacks deserved to be slaves since God had cursed them. Once again, Forrest Wood documents these facts from America's history in *The Arrogance of Faith*.

Even today, you can still hear "Christians" saying all kinds of curses against African Americans. These will not be repeated here in this book. But without understanding, people say what they see with their physical eyes and ears and thus continue the operation of evil in others' lives. The words spoken against African Americans are curses. Christians today are still playing into the hands of the enemy by cursing African Americans.

Even if the words contain measures of truth, the Christian responsibility is to bless and curse not. We cannot expect those who are subject to the enemy to do anything other than his bidding. We are not talking about non-Christians. We are talking about the responsibility of those who claim to know the Lord. Christians are responsible for restoring breaches.

When we think of the fact that these curses are going against African Americans who know the Lord Jesus Christ, it is even more tragic. Members of a body would actually bite and devour other members of the same body.

Derek Prince has done an excellent job researching what the Bible says about curses. The following is a quote from his book *Blessing or Curse: You Can Choose:*

> Both blessings and curses belong to the invisible, spiritual realm. They are vehicles of supernatural, spiritual power. Blessings produce good and beneficial results; curses produce bad and harmful results. Both are major themes of Scripture. As already pointed out, the two words are

mentioned in the Bible more than 640 times. Two important features are common to both. First, their effect is seldom limited to the individual. It may extend to families, tribes, communities or whole nations. Second, once they are released, they tend to continue from generation to generation until something happens to cancel their effects. . . .

This second feature of blessings and curses has important practical implications. There may be forces at work in our lives that have their origin in previous generations. Consequently, we may be confronted with recurrent situations or patterns of behavior that cannot be explained solely in terms of what has happened in our lifetimes or personal experiences. The root cause may go back a long way in time, even thousands of years.

The main vehicle of both blessings and curses is *words* [emphasis added]. Such words may be spoken or written or merely uttered inwardly. Scripture has much to say about the power of words. The book of Proverbs, in particular, contains many warnings as to how words may be used either for good or for evil.

How Can Sins of American Christianity Be Dealt With?

Most people want to keep the part Christians played in creating evil in African American communities under the rug. Many do not want to think about it. Few want to accept responsibility for the current plight in our cities.

Unfortunately, the author of *The Arrogance of Faith* does not take a kind view toward Christianity. Racism among Christians continues to hinder people from seeing the true God. Do we need more mockery because the only Jesus that most Americans have seen has been a false Jesus?

Christians of every color displaying love for each other will give a different testimony to the world. African American women can begin to operate in a radical, unconditional love that will bring change and healing to us, our families and to other members in the family of God. We have an opportunity to demonstrate the true Jesus. Through Christ we can reverse the curse on our families and communities. It will take the Spirit of God to bring conviction and break through the walls of deception.

For most people, the problem of racism and the effects of slavery are someone else's problem. But the sins of the forefathers of American Christianity can be confessed.

We cannot bring the dead back to have them confess their sins. But we can do as Nehemiah did: we can confess the sins of our fathers (Nehemiah 1:6). Some who were wrong were not our physical fathers, but they are still part of our family in the faith. However many of them were our physical ancestors because of the many slave owners who forced slave women to be sexual partners. That glaring wrong needs to be acknowledged as sin and confessed as well.

The sexual abuse against our foremothers still affects us today. We need to break its spell on our lives.

It would be nice if members of the majority American culture took the lead in confessing their sins and the sins of their forefathers in order to begin the process of ridding our communities of their continuing harm. But if no one else is going to do it, we must do it. It affects us too adversely.

"You mean you're not going to talk about what the white man owes us or should do to make things right with us? Shouldn't they at least apologize?" No. You'll have to go somewhere else for what someone else needs to do to solve *our* problems. We have to go to God as the solver of our problems. Our problems are too big for humans anyway. I believe God has all the wisdom we need to bring a restoration to our community.

If God chooses to deal with others and show them things they need to do to make things right, that's fine, but I'm not going to worry myself about what somebody else should do. What good would that do me? Make us feel good?

Let's get our focus off of what others have done. Let's stop waiting for "them" to make it right. It goes beyond what we see in the natural. Spiritual realities are at play, whether it be God or the devil. We cannot wait for others to be the solution to our problems.

Nobody's problems are totally caused by the actions of others. A curse without a cause does not come (Proverbs 26:2). So when others curse us, there are ways of living above it. Our response to others' action is fundamental. God has the power to deal justly with the wrong actions of others if we follow the principles laid down in God's Word.

We have to decide whether or not we will forgive the whites and indeed the African brothers who cooperated with the "man-stealing" of the slave trade. Our response at this critical time will determine whether we will stay in prison or move to the throne room. God can break every yoke of bondage, rooted in the experience of slavery, that has been put on our backs here in America.

Furthermore God has ways of bringing restitution. We must be careful to let God do it in his timing. Our proper response may hasten that time. If we don't want to hear that, we can go ahead and continue to try to get others to change. But if we're serious about seeing some real changes in our communities and cities, we are going to get to some practical ways that we can change and enjoy the blessings of God even if no one else changes.

Rejection and wounds often result in bitterness and unforgiveness. African American women have been rejected much. So in many instances there is an open invitation for the plan of evil to operate in their lives. But this does not have to continue with Christian African American women. We have the privilege of living under the protecting armor of light (Romans 13:12).

The good news is that God is inviting us to get all wrapped up, tied up and tangled up in Jesus. That's what it's all about anyway. We can be keys to change.

Because we have not understood the apparent absence of God's blessing, African American Christians have a rift in our emotions that makes it difficult for us to fully trust the only One who can rescue us from the curse under which our enemy has us.

All of this was planned. "Christians" have been used. The bitter roots among African Americans are a hard-to-unravel web. The solutions many bring to our community only touch the symptoms and never go deep enough. It's time to uproot the roots of evil out of our community.

Our community is entangled in such a mess of sin, lies, curses, bitterness and unconfessed injustices, it will take divine intervention to deal with it all. We should confess not only our sins, but also confess the sins of our natural and spiritual ancestors.

God wants to get at the roots of the problems in our community. In this chapter we have examined the structure of these roots.

The roots of bitterness have been too costly for African American women. It's time to make a transfer back into the hands of God and out of all of the calculated plans of the one who hates our guts because he knows God wants to use us to bring him down.

As I close this chapter I want to remind you that yes, slavery has had a devastating affect on our community. A lot of what you and I go through has been a result. Let's stop giving lip service to God, but rather go to him with our questions. Maybe we'll learn like Joseph, that it was meant for evil, but God has good in store. We'll never know that unless we take our questions out from under the rug.

Questions for Thought and Action

1. Describe some of your ideas about the devil.

2. Discuss your thoughts on the statement, "African Americans may be very religious, but we have a hidden rift with God. We are angry with God." Do you agree, disagree? Why or why not?

3. Read Exodus 3:21-22. How did God redeem the years the Israelites spent in slavery?

4. Could God have known about the slavery of African Americans long before it took place? If he knew, why didn't he stop it? (Read Genesis 15:13-14.)

5. Why is it futile to keep our focus on what others have done to us or should do to make things up to us?

6. Read Proverbs 26:2. What are some common responses to hurt and offense that may contribute to giving place to evil?

7. *Going deeper:* According to Galatians, Jesus has redeemed us

from the curse of the law. Why do we often still suffer from this curse when it was taken by Jesus?

8. Take a moment now to meditate upon and pray aloud this prayer. (If you cannot pray it at this time, perhaps you will be able to at a later time.) "Father, I ask you to forgive anyone who took sexual advantage of the women in my ancestory line. Free me and all succeeding generations from the damage done to us. Amen."

5

the plan against women

• • • • • • • • • • • • • • • • • • • •

*And I will put enmity between you and the woman, and
between your seed and her Seed; He shall bruise your head,
and you shall bruise His heel. (Genesis 3:15)*

I don't like you. I hate your guts. You make me sick. I could kill you.
I could spit in your eyes."

Imagine someone hating you like this and you know that this person's greatest aspiration and desire is to destroy you. Imagine hearing
the above conversation not once, but daily, every minute of the day.
Well, this is the attitude, desire and calculated plan of your spiritual
enemy against you.

The real enemy of African American women has been identified
as a spiritual being, the devil. Here we are going to get to the core of
why he hates your guts: it is because you are female.

You're probably not surprised that he hates you, but you may be
surprised at why. Let me give you a more formal introduction to your
enemy. In fact, I want to take you back to the beginning of time to the
Garden of Eden when we first find him.

God had already made Adam and Eve and put them in the Garden of Eden. In Genesis 3:1 we find our enemy coming on the scene of humanity:

> Now the serpent was more cunning than any beast of the field which the LORD God had made. And he said to the woman, "Has God indeed said, 'You shall not eat of every tree of the garden'?"

Look at that. He comes to the female part of the couple. I wonder why?

According to Genesis chapter 3, this is how the enemy of God tricked mankind over to his side.

*Satan divided mankind by talking only to Eve. Satan knew that dividing weakens the whole. If they had dealt with Satan together rather than Eve dealing with him independent of her spouse, maybe history would have taken a different turn.

*Satan deceived Eve. He lied to Eve about what God had said. Satan insinuated that God was holding out on her and that she could run her own life all by herself. If she knew right and wrong, why would she need God?

*Eve influenced Adam to eat. Adam was not deceived. He knew what he was doing, but he chose to leave God in order to stay with his woman. Women have a tremendous power of influence.

Now comes the reckoning with God. Everybody gets punished. The verse that begins this chapter, Genesis 3:15, tells us Satan's punishment.

The Threat to Satan

As punishment for Satan's part in orchestrating the fall, in Genesis 3:15 we find God threatening the enemy. The Lord God says to the serpent, "I will put enmity between you and the woman, and between your seed and her Seed."

Did you catch that? God said he would put enmity between Satan and the woman. Now we might be tempted to think, *Big deal. I'm sure the enemy is shaking in his boots.* We think very little of the fact that God told his own enemy, Satan, that he would now make women his enemy. In essence, God told Satan "I'm putting woman on you."

The emphasis has always been on the woman's seed. That is critically important. God was speaking of Jesus when he told Satan her seed would bruise his head. But also important is the point about woman herself. Though we may not see it as significant that women and Satan are enemies, Satan has taken it very seriously. God does not make idle threats. Satan knew there was much to the words God speaks.

Satan had a real problem. He is so aware of his problem, he stayed up all night trying to figure out what to do. Before the night was over, he had drafted a letter.

My loyal cohorts,

Did you see what happened in that garden today? Did you see how Eve just held that fruit out to that man and he just took it. She has power! She has influence!

We must see to it that she never teams up with God. The two of them can do our kingdom some serious destructive damage. We must see to it that she does not realize that God loves her, wants to use her or that she is a powerful tool in his hand. We've got to trick, scheme and come up with lies to deceive her. By the time we get finished with her she will be so confused and messed up. And we'll keep her that way, *for life!*

I must warn you. Make sure the woman never knows you are her real enemy. You *always* have to use someone else to do the damage so that her focus is always on them, *not* us. The man is our only hope. Also, be sure the woman never finds out she is our enemy. This is so frightening. If she finds out how much we're scared of her, we're finished!

Your boss,
Satan

P.S. This is a very serious issue. Your very existence depends upon this assignment. I need everyone on board. This will not be easy, but with lies and deception, we can do it.

Women are on the same side as God. We have a common enemy. After the events of September 11, 2001, the day the World Trade Center twin towers were attacked by terrorists, I read in the paper that nations that had the common enemy of the terrorists were now on the same side. Do we want to be on God's side or do we want to be on the enemy's side in opposition to God? It is imperative to see that we are on the same side as God since we both have the same enemy.

A woman teamed up with God is Satan's biggest nightmare. I can just picture him waking up every night, sweating, moaning, screaming because he dreamed we finally found out the truth about him, God's love, our true identity and destiny. Well, I say that nightmare is going to come true. With this book, I hope to be able to help it along.

Notice I said a woman teamed up with God. I did not say a church-going woman. I did not say a religious woman. I did not say a moral woman. In fact, Satan will send you to church, suggest you get religious and help you stay active with all the programs and activities. A good church-going woman is Satan's biggest asset as long as you are not teamed up with God.

You might ask, doesn't going to church mean you're hooked up with God? No! I can't emphasis enough that going to church is not a substitute for a relationship with God. Going to church can be a big deception because one thinks they have it going on with God, but church can just be a place to appease our guilty conscience. The only thing that makes us right with God is initiating and living a life after God's principles.

I mentioned earlier that I have been religious, but I did not reflect God's life. To be active in the things of God and talk about the things of God is easy. But we are told when we know his Word and don't do it, we are self-deceived (James 1:22).

I've been there—self-deceived. Thinking I was hooked up with

God, but my heart was far from him. You can't just be hooked up in your mind and not your actions, God wants everything. It's impossible to be totally hooked up with God when we show we don't really trust him by the very acts of disobedience we display on a daily basis.

I've seen it time after time, nice women, African American women, good women, gifted women, many who serve faithfully in the church, women who look good on the outside but who are broken in pieces on the inside. Our churches are filled with women who think they are pleasing to God, but who don't have a clue about their real spiritual condition.

Getting hooked up with God by becoming a Christian is the beginning to victory. Once a believer, one has to battle constantly to keep living by God's life. The real problem is that we think we're living by God's life, but God knows our heart. The only way we will really find out what's in our heart is to ask God to search it.

When we finish discussing the possible problems of how we ignorantly cooperate with God's enemy, we're going to jump right into how to find out the true state of our hearts. Most who think they have it going on with the Lord will probably be shocked at God's evaluation. But that's the nature of being self-deceived.

But back to our point here. We said a woman teamed up with God is Satan's biggest nightmare. For some reason, God chose women to mete out his strategy against Satan. Women have been given a special assignment to be used of God against Satan. They are chosen vessels. *Satan knows it; he is actually afraid of women, especially African American women.*

It's usually the other way around. Some African American Christian women are afraid of Satan, but not many of us realize that Satan is extremely fearful of us. He is especially afraid of us finding out that he is afraid of us. That would burst his bubble and destroy his plans if we truly knew he has a good reason to be afraid of us. He is afraid that after we find out the difference between a woman walking and living in the Spirit with one who talks about it, we might begin to pursue the walk. Oh, he's having another nightmare!

72

Chosen Vessels

According to the Scripture at the beginning of this chapter, God prophesied a time when the Seed of the woman was going to finally take care of Satan. Satan knew what God said was true. There was no way out for him. Satan knew woman had been destined to be a vehicle for his downfall. It was going to happen. The only question was when. The task was to stop woman from bearing seed.

Let us define the word *enmity*. According to the lexical aide to the Old Testament of the *Hebrew Greek Key Study Bible,* the word *enmity* means to be an enemy, to be hostile to, to treat as an enemy, or to hate. Basically it is a state of hostility. According to *Webster's Dictionary* the definition is as follows: enmity is the attitude of feelings of an enemy of enemies, hostility, or antagonism.

Let us remember it was God who told Satan he was putting enmity between him and the woman. God did not tell Eve that he was putting enmity between her and the devil. He told Satan. God's words to Satan were a curse, a threat.

Though enmity was placed between Satan and women, that is not to say Satan is not also an enemy of men. As men are an ally of women, Satan is also man's enemy. Now, the adversary has a mission to pursue. He now has the insurmountable task of making sure God's threats do not come to pass.

And with that motivation the evil one has put into operation a well thought out plan against women. It was essential for him to do something in order to save himself. Satan figured, "Well, if she is going to be my enemy, I'm not going to let her be the aggressor. I'll strike first, and then she'll always be on the defensive and maybe then she'll never succeed in fulfilling God's plan for her. If she never succeeds in fulfilling God's plan, I'll never be put out of commission." That's what he did. Until now, the deceiver has had a pretty good success rate.

Though the first man and woman were transferred out of the hands of God into the enemy's hand, God threatened Satan that woman would be used as an instrument of his destruction. Satan knows women are valuable in God's sight, so he has tried to get a head start with destructive attacks to the souls and spirits of women. His number one tactic is to place the "beat down tool" in the mind, heart and hand of the black man. We will discuss this further later as we consider how Satan used the enmity that's been placed between him and women and has men and women hating each other instead.

Satan Hates Women

Let me continue to take the lid off of a well-kept secret. The devil reserves a *special* intense hatred for women. We know he hates all mankind. But he has a particular animosity against women. We've seen that the animosity Satan has against women was placed there by God.

Because Satan knows we are key to putting him out of business, he has come up with a special plan to keep us ignorant of our importance. We gain some insight into the adversary's hatred toward all women as we look at his reactions to the woman in Revelation 12:

> And when the dragon saw that he was cast unto the earth, he persecuted the woman who brought forth the man child. And to the woman were given two wings of a great eagle, that she might fly into the wilderness, into her place, where she is nourished for a time, and times, and half a time, from the face of the serpent. And the dragon was wroth with the woman, and went to make war with the remnant of her seed, which keep the commandments of God, and have the testimony of Jesus Christ. (vv. 13-14, 17 KJV)

A woman gives birth to a man child. After Satan is cast to the earth, he persecutes this woman. In verse 17, we read Satan was "wroth" with the woman. It is obvious the devil is angry at this woman and wants revenge. The enmity placed between Satan and Eve was the beginning of an enmity between Satan and all women.

Satan wanted the son the woman was carrying. In Revelation 12:4 he stands before the woman to devour her child as soon as he is born. Satan does not like the fact women can have children. He hates our ability to reproduce.

In Revelation 12:5 John the writer tells us that the man child the woman brings forth is to rule all nations with a rod of iron. The church, the woman in Revelation 12 and women in particular, have a responsibility to raise those who will overcome Satan by the blood of the Lamb and the word of their testimony. They will keep the commandments of God and will have the testimony of Jesus Christ. These are the overcomers.

> And he that overcometh, and keepeth my works unto the end, to him will I give power over the nations. And he shall rule them with a rod of iron; as the vessels of a potter shall they be broken to shivers: even as I received of my Father. (Revelation 2:26-27 KJV)

Just as a woman influenced the first Adam to be independent of God, women have the mandate to influence their children and others to live lives dependent on God. I believe African American women can influence many males and females to become overcomers.

Satan Wants to Destroy Our Seed

Look at two times in the Word that Satan was successful in killing the seed of women. In Exodus it appeared Satan knew ahead of time that a deliverer was going to come forth from a woman's womb to bring freedom to God's people. What did Satan incite Pharaoh to do? He had him try to kill all of the baby boys born to the Hebrew women.

When Mary brought forth the promised Messiah, Jesus, Satan also incited Herod to kill all of the male children from two years and under (Matthew 2:16). Satan does not like the fact that we can reproduce and give our children over to God to be used by him.

Satan is behind abortions. Destinies of many overcomers have been denied by abortions. Think about it, if you consider the two times mentioned above that Satan tried to kill the young. Now think about what has happened since abortion became legal in this country. This marks the third time in the history of the world that a great attack has come against the young; this last time, they don't even make it out of the womb.

This attack is even worse than all of the rest. I wonder why Satan has pulled out all stops to get at our offspring? Could he be afraid of many deliverers coming through our wombs who will put him out of commission?

One strategy against us is to get African American women to physically kill our seed by aborting them. Many of God's chosen vessels have fallen into that trap. I have a friend, Lynne Sajna, who wrote a very insightful book, *Destinies Denied.* In it she details her own experience of two abortions that she had while she was a "good, church-going Christian."

Buying the lie that an abortion is the most convenient option because of our own plans, our education, the stigma or the chance of not getting married only feeds into Satan's design to keep us away from God's ultimate purposes. Lynne Sajna details how much she was sidetracked from God's plans and the subsequent aborting of many other things in her life as a consequence of sacrificing her children to the god of convenience.

To put it bluntly, child sacrifice does not endear us to God but rather gives the enemy place in our lives to drive us further into his camp and suffer more under the consequences he brings. Many chosen vessels have not recovered from the spiritual consequences of that act. Their lives have been one of continual failure and decline.

Many African American Christian women, some very good friends of mine, have fallen into that trap. Fortunately some have been able to get out and have been able to overcome the often severe consequence of the act. Thank God, they did not have to continue to live their lives with the constant failure and decline that Lynne describes as characteristic of her life. I know many other Christian women who still struggle with the aftermath of this serious decision; some don't even know the root of their struggle.

Married with two children, I was pregnant with a third child and because of many other circumstances, I really, really did not want to be pregnant at that time. And even though I knew from Lynne's story that having an abortion can bring major negative consequences, I was in such a bad place spiritually that I let the thought enter my mind. It was truly the grace of God and probably the prayers of many others that helped me dismiss the thought pretty quickly.

One point Lynne has told me is that it is essential that a woman sees her past actions the way God sees them. When we abort a baby, it is murder. We have also participated in child sacrifice/idolatry. As long as we excuse, justify or not really admit to the seriousness of those actions, we will not be on God's side and Satan then will have a place to keep us under his plans. Sometimes true repentance takes place when we get saved, but for some we never quite see what we've done the way God sees it.

But as you understand confession, repentance, agreeing totally with God and renouncing your past actions, you can get free and remain free. The apostle Paul was a mass murderer, yet in his conversion experience he was in total agreement with God's verdict on his actions. You don't see him arguing with God. As he repented fully when he came to Christ, God used him mightily (Acts 9).

It is possible to be free. Jesus paid the price for freedom. Lynne's book has been helpful to many people.

God's plan is for us to train up the next generation. If by God's mercy we somehow missed the trap of aborting our children, we then have another hurdle to cross. We can kill our children another way. Instead of wisdom and kindness on our lips, they contain sarcasm, gossip, slander and criticism. Instead of being instruments of love, joy and peace, we have become instruments of emotional death: strife, anger, bitterness, jealousies, resentments and unforgiveness.

The destructive attitudes that we end up with are helping Satan and his plan. Satan wants our seed. We are destroying ourselves and we are being used as instruments in Satan's hands to bring further hurt and destruction to others. Instead of being tools in the hand of God for good, we are used by Satan for evil.

The end result is what Satan planned all along: broken families. Wounded men and wounded women usually end up separating, emotionally or physically.

After our children are born, the devil will do all he can to make the children we have ineffective against him. He will use our children to cause us some of our greatest pain. If he does not succeed there, he will still persecute us as women just because we bring children into the world.

It is very important to understand that Satan not only hates women and their ability to reproduce, but he is afraid of the authority women have over him. He fears the influence she can be for good in this world. This is the reason that he has so cleverly woven his lies, erected barriers between the sexes and sought to make women feel they are inferior. This enemy of African American women knows when African American women wake up to fight him, his fate is doomed.

The plan Satan has used against women in this world is very similar to the plan he has used against African Americans in this society—breaking spirits with the lie of inferiority. Satan is not very original. The deceiver has majored in telling us what we could not do or be.

African American Women Pay—Even Today . . .
African American women become reactors to the pain inflicted upon them as a result of our enemy's hatred. First, we have fought back in bitterness and anger. Second, we have become passive, accepting the lies of the enemy as truth. Third, we use a subtle method of control over others. By manipulating, intimidating or threatening, women try to maintain a semblance of self-respect while pushing others to change.

The result: we as women are in bondage to ourselves. Instead of living the joyous life of bondservants to a God who cares about us, we blindly follow the path of the flesh and damage ourselves in the process.

. . . But Women Are of Tremendous Value to God
It is worth repeating, God did not make women inferior to men, but rather placed a special value on them. Some women may say, "Well,

if I'm not inferior to a man, why did God seem to put the wife under the husband in marriage?"

Ephesians 5:22-23 says, "Wives submit to your own husbands, as to the Lord. For the husband is head of the wife, as also Christ is head of the church; and He is the Savior of the body." Of course, there are different explanations about what this passage means.

One way of looking at it is for the woman's protection. Since women have been given the mandate to be instrumental in Satan's downfall, they need special covering. Could God have covered her more than the man so that she could be preserved for such a time as this?

Let's imagine that a friend of mine's grandmother owned a beautiful crystal lamp. When her granny passed away she was given one of the posts that went to the lamp to keep. She was told the crystal was very expensive but more importantly it meant a lot to her. As a family heirloom, it becomes very important for you to keep this piece of crystal safe.

Now tell me, would you set this very valuable piece of crystal out on your coffee table or in the kids' toy box? No. You would put it up. You would probably keep it up in a cabinet. More than likely you would cover it to protect it. Valuable things are kept under cover. Valuable documents are kept in safe deposit boxes. Valuable paintings are kept in locked cases, sometimes with hired guards to protect them.

You are probably wondering what all this has to do with what we have been talking about. Well, African American women are very valuable to God. He has a plan for them and until the time of that plan, women have to be protected.

God knew with the advent of sin, selfishness and self-seeking would prevail and men and women would try to control each other. He knew rather than cooperation, rivalry, competition, jealous ambition and all kinds of strife would be present.

The power of influence women had over men had to be brought under structured control. The plan for the woman to be used to defeat the enemy had to be preserved. Thus the woman was placed under the man (2 Corinthians 11:6). It was not based on inferiority, less intelligence or a lower standing on the part of women. To the contrary, she was valuable and as important to God as man was.

Perhaps the word *covering* makes us a little edgy. I personally see it as a blessing. Granted, I have not always seen it this way. In the same passage in Ephesians, Paul exhorts the husbands three times to love their wives even as Christ loved the church. God knew women would suffer more wounds at the hand of the enemy.

I believe as a result of the cross that put aside the curse from the original sin, God was making it very clear that women needed unconditional love in order for their wounds to be healed and for women to walk in their destiny. Why would he tell husbands three times to love their wives if it was not important?

Women are valuable. God has planned for our covering and our healing through love from the same gender that Satan has used to wound many of us. If that's what "being under" means, I don't have a problem with it. But you don't have to take my word for it.

What an awesome God! Slapping Satan in his face by using the same tools for our healing that Satan used to abuse us.

Okay, okay, I can hear many of you beginning to say under your breath, "This lady has really gone off the deep end now." You've been able to hang with me with a lot of my far-fetched thinking. You were hoping I might be right about God's destiny for you as a woman. "If she really expects me to believe that God is going to use males to love us back to wholeness . . . come on now. I don't even believe God can change the males I know."

Ladies, bear with me. God did send Jesus, a male to turn the whole curse around. Is God not able to do the impossible? No, I don't think it will come overnight, but I do believe that God's purposes will stand. As God's Spirit is poured out on *all* flesh, I believe men will begin to walk in their God-ordained purpose as well. God is able! Don't dwell on the seeming impossibility of the situation, dwell on the bigness and goodness of God.

Do we really believe in the God of the Bible? Well, maybe you haven't heard of Martha and Mary, whose brother, Lazarus, was dead for four days, so dead he stank! But Jesus called him forth and he rose from the dead and walked out of the grave. Furthermore, Jesus himself did not come when Martha and Mary called him to come heal their brother. Jesus delayed his answer to them until their brother was dead. You see Martha and Mary already knew he could heal the sick. Jesus wanted to show them something new about himself. He wanted them to know he could also raise the dead.

Now, now. Just wait a minute. Yeah, I hear you. "Mine ain't a Lazarus. He's been dead soooo long, there ain't no meat on them bones to stink." Well, God's got an answer for you too. Remember Ezekiel 37? God gave the prophet Ezekiel a vision of a whole valley full of dry bones. Can you imagine what Ezekiel felt when he looked out at that valley of dry bones? It says the bones were very dry, that means no stinking flesh there.

You think things are hopeless in our community? You think it's impossible for God to use our men to love us back to wholeness? Then maybe you have forgotten what the Word of the Lord spoken by Ezekiel at the command of the Lord will do.

God told Ezekiel to prophesy the Word of the Lord to the dry bones. God himself brought flesh, sinews, skin and breath to dem' dry bones. Let's get close enough to God that we can hear him tell us when to prophesy life to the dry bones we see, or maybe we are currently raising and training a generation of Ezekiels.

I believe God will confront the ingrained lies many African American males believe about African American women and vice versa. I believe God will take down the walls that exist between us. God is intent on bringing them down for his own purposes. Do you believe the God who brought down the walls of Jericho can bring down the walls between males and females? I do.

Single women, don't despair; Jesus is your kinsman redeemer. He is your husband. He is more than able to cover you and love you back to wholeness. And he'll wake up your Adam when he's finished building you.

The Truth

Truth always refutes lies. The truth is African American women, like all women, are extremely loved of God. They have tremendously important purposes to fulfill in our communities and this country. They have the potential to be powerful keys in the hand of God. African American women who learn about God's love and then commit themselves to loving others God's way can change things around for our communities and cities. African American women, they are vessels chosen by God to revitalize our nation.

African American women can take a ride on the real freedom train. There is an underground railroad of truth we can travel to freedom. The truth will set women free. Oh, how the enemy hates the prospect of women realizing what Christ actually did when he liberated them by dying on the cross. Satan never wants us to find out that Christ can live inside us and that there is no distinction between male or female in the Spirit.

A woman is specially equipped with a sensitivity to walking in the Spirit. She has the God-given ability to defend her loved ones from the enemy. She is equipped with extra intuition to know when to pray for her children when they are in danger. She is given a special invitation to come into the throne room to ask God to reverse the damage of the enemy in the lives of her loved ones. There is so much she can do.

Satan has purposely withheld from women the truth of who we are in Christ. He has purposely attacked the position to which Christ has elevated us. Jesus Christ, the one and only true women's liberator!

The Lord wanted the man and woman to become one flesh in order for them to learn unselfish love and also to reproduce more humans to serve him. He wanted them to work together and thus be more than doubly effective than two individuals working separately. The enemy has succeeded in putting a kink in God's plans, at least for a period of time.

Now we're going to see just how valuable women are to God's plans especially for these times.

Questions for Thought and Action

1. Read Genesis 3:1-3. What tactic did Satan first use on Eve? What lie did Satan tell Eve?

2. The author interprets Genesis 3:15 as a threat to Satan. If you were convinced Satan was frightened of you, what difference would that make in how you carry yourself?

3. Discuss how a church-going woman differs from a woman teamed up with God.

4. *Going deeper:* Read Revelations 12:7-17, especially verse 17. When Satan was angry with the woman, who did he make war with? Have you ever seen or experienced anything similar to this? If so, describe it.

5. Proverbs 18:17 tells us the power of life and death is in the tongue. How can we use our tongues to bring life to children (our own, nieces, nephews, children in classroom, in our neighborhoods)?

6. Summarize the key points found under the section titled "The Truth." What are the components of the truth that will refute the lies African American women believe?

7. Describe the experiences you've had to contend with in your struggle with equality between the sexes.

8. As a woman you have tremendous value to God. Take a moment now to meditate upon and pray aloud this prayer. (If you cannot pray it at this time, perhaps you will be able to at a later time.) "Father in heaven, I desire to know the great value you have placed on my life. I ask you to break through any barriers and give me insight in the depths of my heart in such a way that I won't ever doubt it again."

6

african american women: keys to change

◆ ◆ ◆ ◆ ◆ ◆ ◆ ◆ ◆ ◆ ◆ ◆ ◆ ◆ ◆ ◆ ◆ ◆

And it shall come to pass afterward that I will
pour out My Spirit on all flesh;
your sons and your daughters shall prophesy,
your old men shall dream dreams, your young men shall see visions.
And also on My menservants and on My maidservants
I will pour out My Spirit in those days. (JOEL 2:28-29)

Mama! I'm going to be late for school. Why are you just standing here on the porch?"

"Yeah, Mom, we need to hurry. I think I might need you to drop me off at the bus stop this morning. I don't have time to walk now."

"I can't find my keys."

"What do you mean you can't find your keys?!"

"Let me go back in the house and call somebody."

"I'm sorry, but if I can't find my keys, we can't get in the house, we can't get into the car, I can't drive. Nobody is going anywhere. We're all stuck, so we've got to find the keys."

Keys are important. One of the essential keys to stop the destruction we see happening in the African American community is prayer. We've already seen the importance of prayer and the unique place God has given to women in stopping death through prayer. It is an awesome privilege. If prayer were the only key in our hands, it would be more than enough. But God has given us more. There are additional keys to be used in serving God and in influencing families and communities.

God has also given women the key of his Word. When you look at it, prayer and the Word are really two sides of the same coin. In order for an individual to be a woman of prayer, she has to be a woman of the Word. She must be balanced, using both sides of her spiritual brain. The Word of God is the basis for all prayer. Prayer is the key for every purpose God has for women.

African American women need to see being able to read and study God's Word as a gift, a special privilege. When slave traders brought slaves to America, one of the techniques to keep them in bondage was to make sure they did not learn to read. In fact, it was illegal to teach a slave to read and if one was found doing so they were to be severely punished. Here we are a hundred and fifty years later and most of us know how to read. God did not give us this privilege just to advance our careers or finances. God gave us this gift in order that we might read and know his Word.

The woman of prayer and the Word can be a powerhouse in advancing God's kingdom. An intercessor is one who stands between God and mankind: speaking to God about mankind (prayer) and talking to mankind on God's behalf.

I believe I have already made a strong case for how God wants to use African American women to make an impact on this generation for his kingdom. It cannot be overemphasized how important we are to the plan of God. Women have been lied to for so long, many hesitate to come forth to take their place. Other women try to get involved in things that are not for them. They know God has called them to ministry, but are not sure how to do the work of the ministry. Hopefully, understanding God's purpose for women will clear up any confusion.

African American Women in the Purposes of God

God uses women, not to the exclusion of men, but beside men—husbands, sons, brothers, fathers or fellow members in God's family. God uses couples, couples taking dominion over their world and co-operating in tasks God gives. Many African American women who are waiting to enter "the ministry" are already surrounded with numerous ministry opportunities.

God gave both man and woman the task to have dominion over the earth, over the fish of the sea, over every living thing. He wanted them to compliment and compensate for each other. His original plan was for them to work together as equals. That plan has a renewed hope in Jesus' work on the cross.

God is now bringing women to the purposes he had ordained from the beginning. It is imperative women pray. This is not only the means by which we will stop the aggression of the enemy on the human race and storm hell's gates, but it is the means God uses to bring women into his original order.

Referring to Satan, it was promised in Genesis 3:15 that the seed would bruise his head. Colossians 2:15 assures us that "having disarmed principalities and powers, He [Jesus] made a public spectacle of them, triumphing over them in it."

Satan knows he is defeated. But as long as he can lie and trick others into believing that he is not defeated, he'll carry out his plans under the cover of deception. The bride of Christ, the church, has been left here to spread the good news of the enemy's defeat. She has been given the power and authority to enforce what Christ did on the cross.

The only way Satan has been able to continue his work is because African American women and another important woman—the church—has been sleeping on her job. Now when she wakes up, Satan will no longer be able to carry out his work so effectively. In fact, the church has the privilege of cooperating with Jesus until all "His enemies are made His footstool" (Hebrews 10:13).

Let's take a look at a promise in Genesis. "Thou art our sister, be thou the mother of thousands of millions, and let thy seed possess the gate of those which hate them" (Genesis 24:60 KJV). This was a blessing that Isaac's wife, Rebekah, received. Isaac was a type of Christ and Rebekah his wife was a type of the church; this promise is therefore for the church as well. Jesus confirmed it in Matthew 16:18. He said that the gates of hell would not prevail against the church.

In Ephesians 5:21-23 we see the wife is a type of the church. So beginning in the home and extending into the community, women have been given the assignment of defeating the plan of the enemy. This is woman's special place.

Even as women symbolize the bride of Christ, they have some unique roles in God's kingdom. I believe just as Satan targeted women to orchestrate the Fall, God also has targeted women to orchestrate bringing the return of humankind to the original plan of God.

Pouring the Spirit on All Flesh

According to the Scripture at the beginning of this chapter, God promised a day would come in which he would pour out his Spirit on *all* flesh. It appears God wanted to make it clear that the outpouring of his Spirit and the consequent speaking of his Word (prophesy) would include men and women. There is probably little question that we are living in those days. In fact, Acts 2:18-19 lets us know this word has already came to pass. As the book of Acts indicates a beginning of an outpouring of the Holy Spirit, I believe that the days we are living in will represent a torrential downpour on the earth.

The purpose of God's Spirit being poured out on those who know God is to prepare us for our Bridegroom, Jesus. Revelation 19:7 says the Lord's "wife has made herself ready." Jesus told his disciples that the Holy Spirit would be sent to do among other things, teach us and lead us into all truth (John 14:26; 16:23).

From the specific emphasis in Joel of women being part of this move of God, it is obvious that women will have an important place in this army. From the account of God's work among his people, this specific noting of women represents a change. Except for a few exceptions here and there, the Old Testament identifies fewer women then men who God used to speak for him. Many people will point to the culture and societal climate of that time as the real reason. But even taking that into consideration, it still appears that God is not an equal opportunity employer.

Genesis 1:26: "Then God said, 'Let Us make man in Our image, according to Our likeness; let them have dominion over the fish of the sea, over the birds of the air, and over the cattle, over all the earth and over every creeping thing that creeps on the earth.'" After we are told that God created humankind male and female, chapter 2 of Genesis only speaks of the male, Adam. Some time lapsed before Eve was brought on the scene.

I believe we have the same principle in the Word from Joel. God speaks of doing something among males and females. But even in the Acts of the Apostles and the Epistles' accounts of the work of God's Holy Spirit in the beginning of the church, we still see fewer women identified. That's how it has been.

But things are changing. I think it is safe to say that in this last of the last days, we will see a bringing forth of Eve (women) into the scheme of things concerning God's work in the earth. It is God who is doing the change. He told us about it in Joel. It should not surprise us as he is bringing it about.

Change is not always easy. Most of us resist change to some degree. In Genesis when Adam saw he had help, he was delighted (Genesis 2:23). Sometimes tradition (the way it has always been) will hinder males from being delighted to have help. Sometimes the same tradition hinders women from realizing their significant place.

Actually, women have always had a significant place in God's plans, but that place was not always visible. For these times things may be a little more noticeable, but the real issue is not visibility but significance. Some very important roles will always be behind the scene, but a woman must know how critically important she is to God's plans.

As women and men begin to understand what God is doing as his Spirit is outpoured on *all* flesh, both men and women, I believe we will see some considerable change in the ability of the people of God to overcome Satan, our real enemy. As women take their place, it will bring a renewing.

Just as in the book of Acts, the account of the early outpouring of the Holy Spirit on God's people brought forth a people, a corporate group who seemed unbeatable. They overcame threatening, beatings, persecutions, beheading of their leaders, famine, discord between ethnic groups. Likewise, in the days we are living in, I believe the latter outpouring of God's Spirit on his people will accomplish the sanctification and cleansing of the church, making her a glorious, holy church without spot, wrinkle or blemish (Ephesians 5:25-27).

Women as "Birthers" and "Nurturers"

Though there are no female-male distinctions in the spiritual realm, God's Spirit manifests itself through women in unique ways. Much of what God does through women in the ministry of his kingdom correlates to what they have been uniquely fitted to do in the physical realm. For example, only women can give birth. Women are used by God as vehicles to birth new spiritual moves into the earth.

But women do not do it alone. Just as conception does not take place without the seed from a man, likewise the birthing of God's will by women requires cooperation with like-minded Christian men. Instead of competition, there needs to be a harmony that recognizes the unique contribution of both men and women.

African American women are definitely considered nurturers in our culture. You cannot watch a movie about slavery or the black family and not realize her maternal spirit. God wants us to place that on the altar for his use. God desires to use us as a channel of his love and encouragement to those who definitely need it.

Cooperation Is Key

Although African American women can be independent forerunners to change, women and men must work together, complementing each other. Men and women can operate as one unit. When the man is weak, the woman's strength can be there to compensate. And where she is weak, his strength compensates. Tradition and culture will take a back seat here.

When African American men and women strive to work together, the result is less dominating, controlling and manipulating. When Christian men and women learn the proper way of operating together under the one head, Jesus Christ, cooperation can be the rule. As Jesus Christ is in control, unconditional love can erase many of the old ways. Petty jealousies or vying for control will be unheard of in the "new thing."

As women learn to excel in the spiritual arena, giving their lives over to prayer, they can join with men in coruling on the earth. Traditionally some African American men allow Satan to use them as instruments of damage to African American women and children. That's not God's way. As women and men come into alignment with the purposes of God brought back into the earth through Jesus Christ, we will see men fulfilling their God-ordained purpose.

In the home and church community, this purpose is to provide love, cleansing, healing, protection as well as physical resources to females so that we fulfill our destiny (Acts 6:1; Ephesians 4:25; 1 Timothy 5:3; James 1:27). The destiny of men is tied up in the destiny of women.

A woman can certainly choose to serve the Lord on her own even if her household is not serving God. Though it is easier for a man to steer the direction of his home toward God, women can influence the husband to come to the same decision through godly living.

Cooperation with Men, but Intimacy with Jesus

To use another analogy, just as the physical intimate act of sex has to take place before a baby is conceived, so spiritual intimacy with the

Lord Jesus is required for God's will to manifest itself through the lives of women.

Let's take the analogy a little further. Not only has God uniquely designed women to give birth to children in the natural, but he has also fitted them to feed and nurture children, especially in the early years. The mother's milk is the perfect food for a baby. Women have a mothering instinct that serves to care for, protect and defend those who are unable to provide for themselves.

Women are specially equipped for nurturing physically, emotionally and spiritually. If she is a mother, the most important nurturing is to those in her home. If she is not, she still has plenty of opportunities to minister to troubled young people suffering from homes dominated by drugs or otherwise dysfunctional. Children who do not have godly mothers in their own homes are in need of substitute "mothers" who will nurture them.

The process by which children become functioning adults comes largely from the influence of women, mothers, grandmothers and others. Even people besides African Americans have given credit to a black nanny, housekeeper or teacher who strongly influenced their life. Timothy, in the Bible, is a key example of the results of the spiritual nurture received from women in his life (2 Timothy 1:5).

A white female slave owner who mothered children at times would not want to misshape her breasts through breastfeeding so she employed a nursing slave mother to breastfeed her child. The nanny on the plantation often had close ties with the master's children because of the bonding that took place during her nursing time with them and raising them. God used nannies back then to nurture many children.

This is also true in the spiritual realm. God wants to use African American women to care for and protect the new movements that he brings forth. He also wants to use women of color to care for and protect several new spiritual babies.

African American women who do not have young children are called upon to nurture other children through neighborhood Bible clubs, Sunday school and camp. One cannot go too far into our community and not find a child who is in need of extra mothering and guidance.

Women as Keepers at Home

The third important role for women—right up there with birthing and nurturing—is to bring forth and provide a loving foundation for future generations. Titus 2:4-5 alludes to the importance of women loving their children and being keepers of their homes. The word *keeper* used here refers to protection.

The family was instituted in the Garden of Eden as fundamental to healthy life. The woman was instituted as key to the family unit. It is still true that the hands that rock the cradle rule the world.

How does a mother participate in dominion over the earth? She does it by exercising authority over the plans of the enemy. She keeps her family protected from the enemy. She takes authority in the spiritual realm.

And let us not forget every woman has a role in the lives of a number of family members, whether as sister, aunt, grandmother, daughter or niece. In most African American families the grandmother, mother, aunt, someone is seen as the pillar of the family. Once again, God desires to use these natural leadership abilities to bring godly results out of our families.

The enemy is having a field day with our youth. Sometimes your days—or even your years—may seem wasted with sins and mistakes. Well, Jesus can give those years back to us. God promised in Joel 2:25 to "restore of the years that the locust hath eaten, the cankerworm, and the caterpillar, and the palmerworm" (KJV). Every woman can be used of God to defend young ones from the enemy through prayers, attention, instruction and nurturing.

Finally, let us not forget that mothers need "mothering" too. Women who take care of mothers in matters both spiritual and practical help them to better nurture their families. Sometimes a woman's ministry will be to pray for sisters, brothers, cousins and friends so they may become the parents children need.

The African American Woman's Influence

The godly African American woman's method is to influence people. She is able to cooperate with others in proper ways. She fulfills this most important role as she draws close to God. She also demonstrates the pearl of great price, which is a meek and quiet spirit. She gives off a sweet fragrance that indeed influences whoever is sent across her path.

Women of color who are mothers have tremendous influence on their children. As she brings forth new life into this world, a woman is able to provide a healthy environment in which this new life may grow. Through this godly environment, children will have the tools to mature and live their lives in dependence upon God. If mothers would commit to bringing up godly children, praying fervently for them, and teaching and modeling biblical principles, there would be any fewer inner city problems with our youth.

Many of us were raised in a time when our acceptance, even in our families, was based on how we performed. Some of our difficulty in accepting God's unconditional love has been the consequence of performance-based parenting. But as we are changed by God's love, it will change our way of parenting. Our children can more readily be tools in the hand of God for their generation.

The power of influence is one of the most important roles of African American women in both homes and ministry. By example women can influence others to depend upon God. As mentioned in 1 Peter 3:1-5, women can do this without saying a word. Their godly, Spirit-led behavior can win husbands, Christians and non-Christians, over to the Word.

But There Needs to Be Caution

The African American woman's power to influence can be directed toward good or toward evil. That is very important to understand. There is no argument about the power of an African American woman. She cannot be ignored.

Remember when James talks about "praying with the wrong motives"? You have to be careful you do not fall into this category. When you pray, and when you use your influence in someone else's life, please be careful your desires and motives are limited to restricting the power of the enemy and the flesh, not to control another person's will or impose your particular set of priorities on his or her life.

It happens most often in families. When an African American young man is active in the church, many times their mother may want her son to go into the ministry, so she prays toward that end without knowing whether that is really God's will for him. A wife may want her husband to volunteer in one of the church's programs, so she nags him about it until he reluctantly gives in or becomes resentful and aloof. These are examples of the power of influence gone awry.

Women as Teachers

> Likewise, teach the older women to be reverent in the way they live, not to be slanders or addicted to much wine, but to teach what is good. Then they can train the younger women to love their husbands, to be self-controlled and pure, to be busy at home, to be kind, and to be subject to their husbands and children, so that no one will malign the word of God. (Titus 2:3-5 NIV)

A Christian woman teaches other women. She teaches her children. She teaches other children. She instructs with her mouth. She instructs with her life.

Instead of criticizing the young mother who is not feeding the baby right, she offers to help her. She goes by her house and shows her how to fix the formula. She uses her tongue to teach and provide instruction instead of gossiping.

African American women in homes and in neighborhoods need to teach their children to use their anger to fight the real enemy. Women provide protection for their children from evil counsel. By example and instruction they keep their children from harmful practices. They are selective of the things allowed in the home via TV or the toy box.

Women may also teach the Bible to others. As a woman is growing in the knowledge of the Word, she will be given opportunity to share this with others. Older women are to teach the younger women how to be self-controlled, pure, keepers of home, kind and submissive.

Older women pass on to the younger women the wisdom of experience gleaned from past failures and successes. Younger women can thus benefit from the experience of grandmothers. There is a wealth of knowledge that older godly women can pass on to younger women. Much of our struggles can be lighter as we listen to experiences, successes and failures of other women.

Many times one wonders why God did not let people become parents at an older age. Grandparents just seem so much more patient with children. She may be given opportunities to teach in Sunday school, churches, conferences and home Bible studies. Boys' and girls' clubs, backyard Bible classes and other doors may open to her.

Women as Prophesiers
Vine's Expository Dictionary of Old and New Testament Words defines *prophecy* as "speaking forth the mind and counsel of God. It is the declaration of that which cannot be known by natural means. It is the forth-telling of the word of God, whether with respect to the past, present or future."

We will often get a chance to prophesy to the people we pray for. No, not preach at them. We don't mean throwing the Bible at them. We do need to speak God's words of encouragement, comfort and strengthening. That is prophesying according to 1 Corinthians 14:3.

When the newly saved husband comes home drunk, we don't say "How could you do this to me? I thought you were saved." We say "Honey, you're a new creation in Christ Jesus. Old things are passed away. We all make our mistakes. I don't know what happened tonight, but I know God still loves you and I'm going to stick by you."

Instead of telling our children they are no good, we tell them they are an heritage of the Lord and great will be their peace (Psalm 127:3; Isaiah 54:13). That is prophesying.

Speaking encouraging words grounded in the Word is one of the most important keys women have. This godly gift has almost been completely destroyed in many women.

As we study about what the Word of God says about the men and children in our lives, we use it to encourage them. They may not know God loves them. They may not know their sins are forgiven. They don't know God can do exceedingly more than anything they can ask or think. We declare these things to them in their presence.

Sometimes when they are not home, we speak what God says over their rooms. We declare God's Word over them when they are asleep.

African American women will get chances to prophesy in public as well as they are faithful in using the gift in their homes. 1 Corinthians 11:5 specifically identifies women in the public role of prophesying: "And any woman who [publicly] prays or prophesies (teaches, refutes, admonishes, or comforts) when she is bareheaded dishonors her head (her husband); it is the same as [if her head were] shaved" (Amplified Bible).

Women as Rescuers

African American churches are full of women. Good men are certainly needed in the battle against the enemy.

What can we do? We can play a significant role in rescuing our husbands, brothers, sons, fathers, uncles and friends.

Faith without works is dead (James 2:17). God has prepared works for women to do (Ephesians 2:10). Not works to win personal praise from others, but ones others will see and give credit to God in heaven. Lights shining in darkness through good works, a natural overflow of abiding in Jesus Christ, the Light of the world (Matthew 5:16).

Women can be involved in soup kitchens, making clothes for the needy (Acts 9:39), tutoring, hospitality and foster care. Many acts of kindness to others are possible. A smile, a meal, a hug, a ride or a letter are a few of the ways to administer love.

Under Authority, but Also Having Authority

A woman can legitimately say, even as the centurion in Matthew 8:9 said to Jesus, "I'm under authority and I have those under my authority" (paraphrased). As women learn how to be under authority, they can take their positions of authority in the spirit realm.

Though under authority in the realm of the home, in spiritual warfare they have authority to fight and bring deliverance to women, children and men—all those who are touched by their lives.

Women under authority exert authority through prayer, the spoken word and caring acts to effect change over the prisons into which Satan has placed his victims. They will never take a back seat in God's army!

There is a place for women in authority, spiritual authority. As we saw in an earlier chapter God destined women to defeat the enemy. Because of her proposed power over the enemy, she had to be given the most opportunity to be placed under authority. Those under the most authority have the greatest potential to rightly exercise spiritual authority.

We are in positions to use our authority in the spiritual realm over demons, maybe even the demons who have had hold of the very people who have treated us wrong.

As women watch demons go when they tell them, they understand power in the spiritual world is much more important than authority in natural realms. As they realize the purposes of a woman's place, they are thrilled to take theirs in God's kingdom.

Real authority has nothing to do with how many people know us. Real authority has to do with how many evil spirits know us (Acts 19:13-16). The kingdom of God is built completely opposite to the kingdoms of the world. Authority in the kingdom of God is not based upon how many people you have under you, it is based on how many people you have above you to serve.

Matthew 20:25-28 records Jesus saying, "You know that the rulers of the Gentiles lord it over them, and their high officials exercise authority over them. . . . Not so with you. Instead, whoever wants to become great among you must be your servant, and whoever wants to be first must be your slave—just as the Son of Man did not come to be served, but to serve, and to give his life as a ransom for many" (NIV).

God can change our cities if just a few African American Christian women realize their unique value and power and take their authority in the spiritual realm.

Women who truly know God will learn how to practice reverence without fear toward those who take advantage of them. They have seen God deal with others who have been wrong. They know God will avenge them. Their faith in approaching God is filled with confidence.

What are the real issues that cause us difficulty in obeying God in the area of showing reverence to our husbands and other authorities? Is it really because many men are tyrants, chauvinistic, selfish and abusive? Granted this is often the case. We do not want to minimize the difficulty in living under such ungodly circumstances. The enemy has broken many women's hearts at the hand of those with positions of authority. That's part of the plan.

However the real issue is not one of trust in a fallen man who is being used as a tool in Satan's hand. The real issue is one of faith in a good God who is bigger than the devil. The question is not whether our men can hear from God and lead us correctly, the question is whether our God is big enough to make himself heard. Scripture gives witness to the fact that God knows how to talk to people in authority, whether they personally know God or not. "The king's heart is in the hand of the LORD, like the rivers of water: He turns it wherever He wishes" (Proverbs 21:1).

For women, the problem is an unwillingness to wait for God to take our men out of Satan's hands. Patience is our struggle. Trust, obedience and an intimacy with our Father are the real issues. Seeking God first above amicable relationships in our homes, work or school is the bottom line.

When we obey God, God is in a position to speak to those who have been wrong. God does not delight in seeing men crushing women, his chosen vessels. God can deal with fallen men in ways of which we could never dream. As we give reverence to the position of authority (even if we cannot give it to the person), God will honor our obedience.

I'm not talking about physically staying in a situation when your life is in danger or abuse is taking place. Though David was a man after God's own heart and showed the utmost respect to a tyrant boss, even he ran for his life when the spears started flying (1 Samuel 19).

Many women garner admiration from their husbands, sons, brothers, fathers and pastors. But those who don't will not mind. They won't care if they do not receive accolades on earth. They smile, knowing Jesus knows and will recognize them in due time, and give public reward with authority in the new kingdom.

Women have unique roles in the home and in ministry: giving birth, nurturing, defending and influencing family members for good. Women have great potential to turn many people back to a dependency on God.

In this chapter I've continued to give a vision of the possibilities for the future when African American women accept God's call to come up higher and fulfill his purposes.

Questions for Thought and Action

1. Which of the following is true? Explain your choice.

(a) Jesus still has much more he has to do before Satan is completely put out of commission. (b) Jesus has already finished his work. Our part is to believe and enforce his completed work.

2. *Going deeper:* Read Hebrews 10:13, Ephesians 5:21-23 and Matthew 16:18. What do these passages say about who should be winning the battle—Satan or the church of Jesus?

3. Which of the following strategies do you believe Satan has been most successful using and why? (a) scare tactics (b) deception (c) power of persuasion (d) glamour

4. Read Joel 2:28-29 in your Bible noting the context. When Joel predicted a time when the Spirit of God would be poured out on all flesh, why do you think it was necessary for him to specifically mention women as recipients?

5. Do you agree or disagree with the statement that women have always had a significant place in God's plans? Why or why not?

6. Why is it important for men and women to cooperate in God's work?

7. Read 1 Peter 3:1-5. How are women to win their husbands?

8. Take a moment now to meditate on and pray aloud this prayer (if you cannot pray it at this time, perhaps you will be able to at a later time): "Father, I want to fulfill the destiny for which you chose me. Let the outpouring of your Spirit be on my life. Transform me and conform me in the image of Christ. Let my life be used to manifest your character and presence."

part 3
back to the beginning

7

the real enemy

◆ ◆ ◆ ◆ ◆ ◆ ◆ ◆ ◆ ◆ ◆ ◆ ◆ ◆ ◆ ◆ ◆ ◆ ◆

*How you have fallen from heaven, O morning star [Lucifer],
son of the dawn! You have been cast down to the earth,
you who once laid low the nations! You said in your heart,
"I will ascend to heaven; I will raise my throne above the stars of God;
I will sit enthroned on the mount of assembly, on the utmost heights of the
sacred mountain. I will ascend above the tops of the clouds;
I will make myself like the Most High." But you are brought down to
grave, to the depths of the pit. Those who see you stare at you,
they ponder your fate: "Is this the man who shook the earth and made
kingdoms tremble, the man who made the world a desert,
who overthrew its cities and would not let his captives go home?"*
(ISAIAH 4:12-17 NIV)

I received the following in a letter from a young lady I had known a few years back who had many struggles as a Christian:

I started stealing at twelve. I aborted my son at thirteen, I started using drugs at fourteen. I married at nineteen. I was an adulteress right away. I even lived with another man for a time while married. I left my husband when I was twenty-six. I have experimented with group sex involving both men and women. I have had, at times, more than one man a night. I have had sex in public. I have slept with over sixty men in this lifetime. I have gone to every kind of club, juke joint and disco in the country. I have lied, deceived and hurt people. I have used people, partied myself into a near coma, and tried to fool God. I have tried to hide from God and blamed everyone, including Him for my problems.

But I am here to tell you . . . today I have accepted Christ and I am finally turning my life over to the Lord in a real way. I am so glad! I am so excited. I am so relieved! It has been a long and rough journey. I am sure the journey I have ahead will be longer and harder still. But I am confident in Christ that it would be both rewarding and fulfilling. I am so excited and eager about the adventures that lie ahead. I didn't write what I wrote earlier as a plea for sympathy or pity or even prayer. I write to testify to the sheer power, mercy, goodness and infinite love of our Lord Jesus Christ.

God is delivering me and all that I am from myself. He is making me see the magnitude of all that I am and all that I have done. How much more a sinner can a person be? Yet, God is changing me. It is truly remarkable. In spite of everything, I can look forward to a life of awesome testimony for the Lord. That is why I am so excited. I can empathize with the abused child, the sexually promiscuous women, the child aborter, the drug addict, the liar, the deceiver and a host of others who are lost to Christ in the same manner that I was.

Even with all that I've done, God has gifted me with remarkable abilities. I am articulate, intelligent, personable, creative, and so many other possibilities. And now, through Christ, I am learning to adorn the armor of Christ. I am learning about how to use the spiritual tools He has placed before me. I am so excited to think of all I can do!

Sometimes it may appear God is against African American women because of many of the painful things we experience. God is not against us; he is for us. If we understand spiritual laws, we can see why things happen the way they happen.

You have already been made aware that we do have an enemy. Now we're going to unwrap his cover. This enemy is not to be glorified. I do not wish to talk about him in such a way that he is exalted. But he is real. There are a few things we need to know about him in order to make sure we're not on his menu for supper.

This enemy is a spiritual being. He goes by a number of names;

the devil is probably the most common. But Satan is the one I use most. Satan was first an enemy of God before he became the enemy of humanity. Let's go to the very beginning. We'll start with God.

God is *the* positive spiritual reality. God was before time and is beyond time. He created time, the earth and all that is in the earth. God is above all and it is by him that all things exist. He currently holds up everything by his Word (Hebrews 1:3). God is awesome. He's everywhere all at the same time. God knows everything. He sees everything.

Look, ya'll, God knows the number of hairs on your head, even the nappy ones (Matthew 10:30). He takes care of all the birds of the air (Matthew 6:26). God is *big!* Did you know the earth is God's footstool? (Isaiah 66:1) He ain't no weakling who don't know what he's doing and can't carry out what he promises. God spoke and brought the worlds, the galaxies, including all the planets, into existence (Genesis 1). That's the kind of God I'm talking about.

So the first thing you need to know about the enemy is that he "ain't" God. The second thing you need to know about the enemy is that God is so far above him and so much bigger, that it really is not a comparison. The next thing you need to know about the enemy is that Jesus Christ as a man already brought him down. You and I only enforce what was done on the cross. That's all you really need to know. These other things I'm going to tell you are just to help you stay away from his deception. He's a liar, so I'm going to tell you some things ahead of time so if he lies to you, you'll recognize it.

Satan

In the time before time was, there was only God. At some point, God created beings that are called angels. Satan was one of the created beings, an angel.

Satan, holding a high position in God's kingdom, decided he wanted to take God's place. He persuaded one-third of the angels to side with him as he led a mutiny in heaven (Revelation 12). Anyone in serious conflict with the King of the kingdom does not belong. Furthermore it was impossible for a created being to be over the Creator, the One who always was. As a result God had to kick him out of his kingdom (Luke 10:18). In fact, he was sentenced as a punishment for his insubordination; but his sentence was not immediately carried out.

Satan wanted to replace God. He does not want any of God's purposes to work. He's the real enemy of mankind. He is God's enemy too. Since we have the same enemy as God has, we are technically on the same side as God.

This enemy of God is still waging a losing battle against God. Though the two are in conflict, there is really no contest between them. It's even worst than an ant trying to subdue an elephant. God and the devil are not even in the same league.

As much as we would like to deal with things we can see, behind many of our problems is an army of unseen personalities. The commander in chief, the same one who tried to overthrow God, is a deceiver. In opposing God, he has become the negative spiritual reality.

You see if the conflict between God and Satan were direct, there really would not be a match. However the conflict is indirect and dependent upon the responses and cooperation of a third party. That third party is us—humans.

Where do humans come in? Some time after God created angels, he created humans to be objects of his love. Humans, with a free will that Satan works diligently to manipulate, are the center of the conflict between God and the adversary.

The deceiver is jealous. He hates humans because they are made in the image of God and have the potential of becoming corulers with the Son of God, Jesus Christ. He knows we were created with the ability and destiny to defeat him. That's what he does not want you and me to find out. He does not want us to walk in our God-ordained destiny.

An important fact: God is good and only desires the very best for all his children. African American women especially need to see how the deceiver has lied about the goodness of God. We will go behind the scenes and look at how the enemy keeps us from the blessing of God in order to make God look bad.

African American Christian women need to realize our real enemy. And even as Satan is our real enemy, God is our friend. Even if God allows Satan to do what we would consider "evil," God may have purposes that we know nothing about. God is a good God, a just God. As we learn his ways, which by the way are higher than ours (Isaiah 55:8), perhaps we will stop trying to figure out good and evil on our own.

If we learn to walk in the Spirit, we can begin to reverse the curse that Satan endeavors to keep over our lives. We can see that Satan is our enemy, and we can begin to cut our ties and relationship with him as we evict him out of our lives.

Your Enemy Is Not Who You Can See

Because Satan is invisible, we do not see him. We only see the people he has used to cause pain in our lives. But they are just hammers in his hand. We've been mad at the hammers while we have left Satan alone. African American women beat up on hammers while Satan has slipped away and not felt a single blow.

Imagine, for example, that someone hits you. Imagine he uses a hammer to do so. Then imagine that you take the hammer, throw it on the ground and stomp on it.

"Stupid," you say?

The person who hit you would be happy. He may realize that you were terribly misinformed, but he wouldn't tell you.

When we focus our anger against people, it is like focusing on the hammer. Satan often uses people to carry out his plan of attack. Many even allow themselves to be used of the enemy. But for the enemy it serves as a trap to get us bitter at the person and into enemy territory. People are not our enemies. Ephesians 6:12 is very clear on that:

> For we do not wrestle against flesh and blood, but against principalities, against powers, against the rulers of the darkness of this age, against spiritual hosts of wickedness in the heavenly places.

Someone could use a hammer to hit us on our head, but it would be ridiculous for us to be bitter and hateful toward hammers the rest of our lives—perhaps a little cautious, but not bitter. Hammers can also be put to good use.

What we need to understand is that Satan is the real enemy of African American women, *not* males, whites, or God. Satan has used males and whites to hurt us, but because they have been used does not mean they are our enemies.

Let's focus our anger on the real enemy. Let's get our minds off the hammers. We need to recognize that everything done to us was done under the direction of the enemy. But we also need to realize that God can still make good out of it.

Let's turn our anger in the right direction. God can help us do it right.

I guess the most important realization I have made over the last ten years since I first wrote *Chosen Vessels: Women of Color, Keys to Change* is that African American women have problems identifying their friends and their enemies in the spiritual realm. Many of us treat God as our enemy and Satan and his cohorts as our friends.

Unfortunately we have fallen into Satan's plans instead of pursuing God's purposes. It takes effort, energy and change to pursue the purposes of God, but it takes little or nothing to fulfill Satan's purposes. In fact, we can be as religious, church-going, Bible believing, Bible quoting, tongue talking as we want to be and still not be in God's purposes if we treat God as our enemy and his enemy, Satan as a friend.

Sleeping with God's enemy? No! No way. God help us make the transition.

A Closer Look at the Enemy

Satan is a liar and is the father of lies (John 8:44). The truth is not in him. However, he does have an advantage: we often believe the lies he has to say concerning God and what is good for us.

Satan is also a spirit. We cannot see him but he is very real. He operates behind the scenes, and is clever at getting his job done. His main talents are trickery and deception; he is a master magician who specializes in delusion.

Unlike God, Satan cannot be everywhere at the same time. Therefore the deceiver has a lot of help to carry out his plans. He has a well-organized army doing most of his work. It is unlikely Satan himself would personally pay attention to any of us. But his capable helpers, who are the angels who joined with him in the rebellion against God, are great in number. They carry out Satan's plan, using his tactics. The helpers are called evil spirits or demons. When I say what Satan does, it is usually one of his imps that actually carries out the plan. We just use his name because he is the mastermind behind it all.

More than one demon may be assigned to each of us as part of the enemy's plan to get us away from God. (We have good angels that did not rebel assigned to us too! See Matthew 18:10.) These assigned demons know us from our birth, they catalog our weaknesses and plan how to arrange circumstances to make us angry and rebellious toward God. They know the kinds of attitudes and behaviors that already have the judgment of God. They try hard to make us act in ways to bring us under their influence and out from under the protecting hand of God.

Disobedience and fear, the opposites of trust and obedience, attract these unholy angels. They know us so well, it is easy for them to use circumstances and people to get us to stop trusting and obeying God. They know what makes us fearful, irritated, independent and essentially what moves us away from God, our friend, and into Satan's territory.

The "Germ Theory"

I watched a video about hand-washing techniques for hospital workers several years ago, and an idea struck me. Satan and his helpers are like germs. They infect people, but can be "washed away" with the right techniques.

In the physical world germs are everywhere. But how many of us are preoccupied with them? We do not get concerned about germs until our own defense system is weak. Of course, we are more susceptible when we are in the presence of someone who is infected and is spreading their germs by coughing or sneezing. Under these conditions, we try to protect ourselves.

The same can be said for "spiritual germs." They are everywhere. Jesus is the only defense against "spiritual germs." Any person who has not received him is infected already. A person who knows him but is not walking close to him has their defense weakened.

The earth is full of people infected with "spiritual germs." These people are sick and need a Physician. The people of God have been given the commission to bring them healing. God's people have been given whole warehouses full of the antibiotics of truth to cure spiritual infection. God's people have been given the mandate of demonstrating germ-free living and introducing people to the Physician, Jesus Christ.

Normal, spiritually healthy people have nothing to worry about concerning evil spirits. Those who are spiritual babies, young, spiritually sick or who have wounds in their soul do have to worry about becoming infected with spiritual germs. Also those who work in places that have a high density of infected people need to practice good hand-washing techniques!

Passing Germs Around

God's goodness is available to those who remain close to him; God's wrath comes to those who stay close to the enemy. Those who stay at a distance from God, away from his hand of protection will experience evil consequences from the enemy. God's protection is lifted when we walk with or are "sleeping with the enemy."

Even people who have invited God into their lives are prone to wander from God's presence. We are prone to act independently and control our own lives. Independence from God is sin. Moving away from God leads to sins, the activities that either hurt us or others such as lies, hatred, murders; you know the list.

Like fear, sin also invites spiritual germs. Sin puts a hole in the armor of a Christian, giving the enemy an open door to our lives and often to our descendants. Once Satan has a person under his bidding to act in opposition to God's best, that same germ can pass down through four generations (Exodus 20:5). This is how the sins of parents are passed on to children. All sin hurts somebody.

The enemy's plan has been to infect as many people with as many germs as possible, getting a better grip on the human race. The enemy also influences people to sin against others. That's another one of his ways of passing germs around. These evil acts build up and eventually release the judgment of God. That is what the enemy wants.

In the physical arena a wound will give germs more opportunity to spread and do damage. One of the enemy's most successful ways of hurting humans is their ability to operate through others to bring abuse. Once a person is wounded emotionally, the environment is now conducive to germ/evil spirit infestation. So when Satan uses a "hammer" to wound us, he is hoping for an inroad into our life.

Bitterness, unforgiveness, resentments will give evil that access. Before we know it, we'll be instruments for someone else's wound. That's how it works. It's all a set up. As much as we have heard about letting go of bitterness and forgiving people for the wrong they have committed, we still think we have a right to disobey God in these areas. We do have a choice; we don't have to do it God's way, but then we can keep our pet demons if we want to as well. It's really our choice, African American sisters.

I've been guilty of just shaking my hand and saying, "I just can't believe that young lady is acting like that. Why, I know her mother didn't bring her up that way. What's wrong with her?"

Well, did you know sexual sin is one of the most effective ways of spreading spiritual germs from one person to another? Most of us have heard about the dangers of sexual impurity, but many do not understand why this particular sin is so devastating. It is especially warned against in the Word of God. The warnings are not meant to reduce our fun but rather to protect us from physical disease as well as from the enemies of our souls.

A little girl forced into a sexual relationship without her consent will still have the demonic aftermath. Many of these girls become promiscuous as teenagers. The promiscuity was probably driven by those demons that may have lain dormant for years. When we know these things, it should help us in the way we treat those who suffer sexual abuse. It also should help us know how to assist the one who struggles much in these areas. Demons can be evicted.

How Satan Gets a Foot in the Door

Once I mistakenly left the back door of my apartment unlocked. A boy who lived in the building came in and stole some things. Most of the things were recovered. But I did not know the boy had also stolen a spare back door key.

The key gave the boy access to the apartment. When we were away from home, the boy came in and stole more things. Once it was discovered he had a key, the locks were changed and the stealing stopped.

The enemy can get into our lives when we leave a door open. We can do this by allowing an accumulation of unconfessed sin in our lives. When Jesus himself is not the sole key to our hearts, the enemy can use those other things to which we give our hearts as access in and out of our lives. We will shut the door on the enemy and change the locks as we learn to remain close to God.

God has provided safety for us from the enemy. It could be compared to being in the center of a corral with God. As long as we stay right next to him, in his lap, we're safe from the enemy.

The enemy resides on the other side of the safety fence but is always trying to attract our attention. Often we are deceived into thinking the other side of the fence has good things. Sometimes we'll even get down out of God's arms to get a closer look and end up falling into trap of the enemy. Soon it is a stronghold and becomes harder to come back to God.

Many times when others upset us, we don't see that God is on our side, cleansing us, building our character, showing us things about himself, in spite of the injury. We look at things from the viewpoint of what is convenient or comfortable for us. We just look at the fact that we now have an injury. Instead of cleansing it, putting on antibiotics, covering with clean bandages, we baby our injury, exposing it to dirt and grim, allowing infection to set in.

When things don't make sense, we drift from God. God wants to be our help and refuge. We need to be running to get under his wings. We need to learn how to jump into his lap. We've got to do it God's way.

Can Christians Be Infected?

That is a controversial question. The Scriptures tell us not to give place or ground to the enemy. The Scriptures tell us the enemy can aim wiles at us. They say that as we restore others, we should look to ourselves lest we also fall. They tell us to take our thoughts captive, casting down imaginations and strongholds (2 Corinthians 10:5; Galatians 6:1; Ephesians 4:27; 6:16).

Obviously, the enemy can work in the lives of African American women to make us weak and ineffective, even put us to sleep. It is also obvious Christians have a responsibility to stay clean.

It is possible for Christians to become infected with the thoughts of the enemy. These thoughts give the enemy access into our lives. When we allow thoughts that enter our minds to stay and become a way of living; we have a stronghold that needs to be disinfected.

My daughter, Esohe, is a freshman at the University of Michigan as I am writing this. Back when she was just a toddler and we lived in Chicago, I remember a time when Esohe saw a friend of ours coming to visit. Before anyone knew what was going on, my daughter ran across the street to meet our friend. A car came within an inch of her life.

We were all very glad and grateful to the Lord that she was not hurt. After my heart settled down, I began to get fearful. You see at the time, God had led me to pursue him very seriously. After I had first decided to pursue God with my all at the age of seventeen, I almost died. I had learned that Satan does not take kindly to the thought of an African American woman pursuing God. But by that time, I had learned that God was bigger than the threats of Satan in my life.

But now he was messing with my baby girl. I did not want to put my children in jeopardy because of my following hard after God. I could handle myself, but it did not seem fair to subject my children to Satan's threats, no matter how idle they were.

The wile Satan threw at me through one of his imps was encased in fear. I'm sure from observing my life, they knew my tendencies toward fear. The thoughts implanted in my mind went like this: "So you still want all God has for you? Look how close I came to taking your little girl. Keep this God thing up and I won't miss next time. Is God really worth your precious little girl? You really don't have to be so serious about God. Look around you. You can still go to church and be religious without getting fanatical about it. Lighten up. It won't hurt to slack up a little. In fact, it might help keep your children safe."

You know what? I gave some serious consideration to his offer. In fact, I slacked up for a bit. I'm not sure how long it was. But God finally got my attention and exposed the enemy's lie for what it was. And I got back on track. But time was lost.

Another trick of the enemy in my life is to get me to worry about my reputation. At times, God will be prompting me to do or say something and I hesitate because the thought comes: *What will they think about me?* It all goes back to fear, the fear of man. Fear has been a stronghold in my mind that the enemy can use to talk to me.

It has been needful for me to continue to disinfect that route/access to my mind the enemy uses. If we fail to disinfect properly, the enemy can come in and out of our circumstances, stealing, killing and destroying. He steals our joy, peace and right ways of living. He brings his garbage with him, leaving it at his will.

It starts in the mind. God says we are to live in the power of his Spirit. But too often we find that our lives are motivated and energized by our mind, will and emotions—our souls.

The Word of God washes us. The word God has given me on the fear of man is found in Galatians 1:10. When I'm battling in my mind whether to obey God or succumb to the fear of man, God begins to speak to me: "You can't be my servant if you still try to be a man-pleaser." Eventually, the Word of God washes away the fear. I'm good to go . . . until the next time.

God wants us to acknowledge him in all our ways. If we try to "do the right thing" by our own understanding, without acknowledging God in all our ways and diligently seeking his face, we are living from our minds without the help of God's Spirit. This inevitably leads to sin.

There is no fear in God. In fact, God's Word tells us in 1 John 4:18 that perfect love casts out fear. The fear was not from God's Spirit. The fear was a part of my past experiences that got stuck in my mind.

To say that the enemy cannot get into our lives is a lie serving the enemy's purposes. The enemy can have place, ground and even a stronghold in our lives. We can suffer from his wiles. We can fall into his traps. As I indicated before, African American Christian women, you can have a demon if you want one. I don't like them, so I'm trying to get rid of all mine.

Faithful African American women *can* be infected. Spiritual germs do not have legal right to reside in a believer's body or soul. Evil spirits have legal right to attack us when we sin, and legal right to reside in unbelievers. Even though they do not have the legal right to live in us, they try anyway. They do not necessarily follow the rules. And when we do not know our inheritance, they take advantage of our ignorance. God's people are destroyed for a lack of knowledge (Hosea 4:6).

If we refuse to fill our lives with God's presence, some can definitely move in as nonpaying tenants until evicted!

No, evil spirits do not belong in blood bought vessels of Jesus Christ! But mice and roaches will try to stay in a house as long as no one challenges them. They will also hide their presence to keep from getting exterminated.

Satan does not like us to have access to truth. He hates truth because it destroys him like boiling water melts ice. When we walk in truth, the enemy's plans are thwarted.

Though the enemy is very clever, he has no power, except what is given him. Christians have been given power over the enemy and his kingdom. Those who know Christ have the mandate of destroying the devil's works and maintaining his defeat.

Being a Christian does not guarantee victory over Satan, especially if we are ignorant of Satan's techniques. We can give up the victory purchased for us by neglecting to forgive, participating in activities that attract evil, trying to live our lives by our own understanding and by refusing to put on our armor. The real danger is trying to live for God with rebellion in our hearts.

The enemy is not able to trick one who stays in the presence of God. The way has been provided for us to live above all of the evil one's strategies. In this sense, victory over the enemy has been guaranteed by Jesus Christ.

How Do We "Disinfect"?

There are many ways of getting rid of unwanted germs. The water of the Word cleanses. Remember my personal illustration. Fiery trials also burn out germs, much like fever. We can change the locks on our hearts by letting Jesus alone be our heart's desire. African American Christian women need to disinfect our minds with large doses of the antibiotic of truth. We learn to take regular spiritual baths (confession). We need to learn how to eat properly (Bible reading, study and meditation). We all need the continuous flow of the blood of Jesus in our lives to fight infection and provide immunity to germs.

Are you severely infected? Perhaps fasting and prayer will get you started on your way to renewed spiritual health (for extended fasts of more than a day, be sure to consult with your doctor, especially if you have any physical ailments). Can you imagine the spiritual revival that would begin to take place in our community if a few (it does not take many) African American Christian women decided to get serious with God? What would happen if we diligently fasted and prayed and sought the Lord through his Word and allowed him to cleanse us totally of all those old thoughts and ways? The day of Pentecost as in the book of Acts would happen not only in our communities but around the world.

Satan's power and ability was stripped at the cross of Jesus Christ (Colossians 2:13-15). That's the good news most of us need to know. The Word of God and the Holy Spirit are available to maintain the reality of what Christ did at the cross.

The Bondage Breaker by Neil Anderson is a good book to read if you want to know more about becoming free of spiritual germs.

In any case, let us get rid of the deceiver's plans against our lives. Let us be careful not to leave any "flesh hooks" for him to grab as we take back the ground we have given him.

The enemy can introduce evil into the lives of people in several ways. He can gain access to our lives by the actions of our ancestors. He can occupy ground that we personally have given him. He can steal the key to our hearts and use it to come in and out at will.

When we sin, he can get through the hole created in our armor. As we saw in the beginning of this chapter with the hammer illustration, when he cannot get to us directly, he can work through the people around us or in our circumstances to cause us to be bitter, frustrated or lack faith in God.

We've talked enough about the enemy. Let's go back to the beginning and see God's original purpose for humankind. It's God's side we are on and want to stay on. Next, we will examine the creation of people and our make-up to give us additional insights of how to stay close to God.

Questions for Thought and Action

1. Read Isaiah 14:12-15 in your Bible, noting the surrounding context. Read it in at least one other Bible version. Who wrote the passage? Who were the recipients of the passage?

2. Which of the following traits does Lucifer exhibit in Isaiah

14:12-17? (You may select more than one.) Show how he demonstrates the trait or traits you select. (a) self-will (b) pride (c) lying (d) rebellion (e) anger (f) fear (g) hate

3. The author speaks of sin as one of the things that attract evil spirits. Describe an instance in your or some one else's life in which an act of disobedience to God opened a door to the enemy ability to steal.

4. How does Satan capitalize on emotional wounds?

5. Read Ephesians 4:27; 6:16, Galatians 6:1-2 and 2 Corinthians 10:5. Match the verse with the admonition.

Consider yourself._____

Bring every thought into obedience._____

Don't give ground to the enemy. _____

Quench the enemy's firey darts. _____

6. Which of these admonitions do you need in your life?

7. *Going deeper:* Identify a stronghold in your thought life. Find a verse that counteracts the stronghold.

8. If victory over the enemy has been guaranteed by Christ, why is it that many Christians do not experience that victory?

9. Take a moment now to meditate on and pray aloud this prayer (if you cannot pray if from your heart at this time, perhaps you will be able to at a later time: "Father, I believe your Word that Satan has already been defeated. I don't know if I've given him place in my life, but I do know I don't want him to have any ground in me. I give you permission to convict me of erroneous thinking. Wash me with the water of your Word."

8

the creation of humans & their fall

• •

Then God said, "Let us make man in Our image,
according to Our likeness; let them have dominion over the
fish of the sea, over the birds of the air, and over the cattle,
over all the earth and over every creeping thing that creeps on the earth."
So God created man in His own image;
in the image of God He created him;
male and female He created them. (GENESIS 1:26-27)

et's say we are convinced that we need a new manager for our lives. What would we want? We would look for someone who would know the job, who had a lot of experience, who was available and who we could afford.

Well, someone wants the job. God has forwarded his resume to us: the Bible. Why don't we go over a brief synopsis of his qualifications and give his offer some serious consideration?

GOD

Dear Friend,

I heard you were considering a new manager for your life. I would like to apply for the job. I believe that I am the most qualified candidate. I am the only One that has ever done this job successfully. I was the first manager of human beings. In fact I made them, so I know how humanity works and what is best to get people back into proper working condition. It will be like having the manufacturer for your personal mechanic.

If this is your first time considering me, I would just like to point out that my salary has already been paid by the blood of my Son, Jesus on the cross of Calvary. What I need from you is the acknowledgment that the price is sufficient to pay for all of your sin and your independence from me. I need you to believe this in your heart and to tell somebody else about your decision with your mouth.

The next thing I ask from you is the right to change and fix your life so that you learn how to stay close to me. I will make some major changes and revisions. They are not for you to worry about. I need your permission to execute these changes in my way and in my time. I will change your desires and I will give you the strength to make the changes. Please keep your hands out of the way. Don't try to take charge of what I'm doing and don't resist me. I really do need your full commitment and total cooperation. If you give me those, the process can go smoothly, without delays.

Yours sincerely,
GOD

P.S. I AM. I created the heavens and the earth. I CAN!

GOD

RÉSUMÉ

Experience: Before the beginning of time. From everlasting to everlasting.

Ability: All-powerful.

Prior Employment: Created the universe, put the galaxies in place, formed man. Established heaven and earth by my spoken word and currently holding up the world by my power.

Education and Training: Have *all* knowledge, am *all* knowledge.

Character References: Overall, my character is love, light and life (John 14:6; 1 John 1:5; 4:16). A representative but by no means conclusive list of other character traits follows:

Wisdom	James 1:5
Comfort	1 Corinthians 1:3
Truth	John 8:32; 14:6
Healer	1 Peter 2:24
Strength	Philippians 4:13
Forgiveness	1 John 1:9
Provider	Philippians 4:13
Mercy	Ephesians 2:4
Just	Romans 3:26
Good	Matthew 19:17
Peace	Romans 14:17

Availability: Willing, able and ready to take over your life. Able to put your life back together again. Will bring all of who I AM into your life. Can start now. Will transform your life if you let me.

Salary requirement: Work in your life has already been paid for through the blood of my Son, Jesus. Your only payment is to commit initially and on a daily basis to trust and obey what Jesus has done and wants to do in your life.

We would do well to let God take over our whole lives. We have made a mess trying to manage them on our own. Even those of us who have invited him into our lives really need to let him take full control.

The whole issue is one of control. The problem we have with God is we would rather keep control over our own lives, while God requires being in complete control. God wants control because that's the way he made us to function. He waits for us to give it to him.

God formed (created) mankind in his own image. He had great plans for mankind. He created a world that was good. He gave so much to Adam and Eve, the first couple. This was all because he loved them so much. They were his own. As the perfect Father and the best example of a loving father, he only desired the very best for them.

Black babies seem to always be born cute, with a full head of hair, a smile and a personality. But get that baby home and they are just like all other babies, crying, wanting their needs met, not concerned about your sleep. They may cry while you are attempting to enjoy the church service. We all come here demanding our own way.

At some point in our lives we gave over our will for God to remold and remake us. Or wait a minute. Did we, Christian sisters? Are we still crying and screaming, demanding our own way? Have we allowed Christ to be truly the Lord (captain, inspector, director and leader) of our hearts and lives?

It was necessary that mankind be made with a free will. If they were forced to only comply with the will of God, they would not love or obey God from a position of freedom. Their will had to be their own.

Now, when God made mankind, he made them to be dependent on his life. God intended that mankind would be a reflection of his glory in everything they did. God gave mankind dominion over the whole earth, over every creeping thing. This dominion did not mean God was no longer in charge. He just gave the overseeing of the earth to Adam and Eve. They in turn were to carry out their job by depending on God in their relationship with him.

Mankind was created to be dependent upon God. Adam and Eve were not only made in the image of God, but God also made them with his breath.

When God made mankind in his image, he made them as spirit beings. In fact, the spiritual part of mankind came from God.

The Lord God formed mankind out of the dust of the ground and breathed into that form the breath of life. This breath of life was the life of God, man's spirit. Humankind's essential essence is spirit. But that spirit was placed in some dirt.

However, God did not want humans to just be spirit beings in heaven with him. God had created the physical environment, the earth and all the trees, grass, mountains, animals, oceans and seas. This was where he chose for people to live. (We see the account of God creating the earth in Genesis 1.) In order for humans, who in essence came from God the Spirit being, to live on the earth, God made a house for human spirit to dwell. Some people call this house our body, an earth suit.

Our spirit came from God. Our human body came from the dust of the earth. Now when the breath of God hit the dirt, the soul came forth. It tells us man then became a living soul (Genesis 2:7). The combination of God's breath with the ground created this third part of man, his soul.

Actually, the Hebrew word for "living" is the same word used for God's breath. God's breath became man's spirit. Essentially man became a spirit/soul. The spirit and the soul are so close that it is difficult to distinguish them from one another. Some people put the soul and spirit together as the immaterial part of humans and only identify two parts to our being: (1) spirit/soul and (2) body. Actually, I can see it this way too.

Even though we separate the spirit for the sake of clarifying some things, I still believe humankind is spirit/soul. Some will say we are a spirit, we have a soul and we live in a body. I personally would say that we are spirit/soul that functions in the physical realm through a body.

In the beginning, the essence of a human being was spirit, but this spirit had soul attributes. With the soul, humans relate to each other and are identified as unique individuals. Actually, I believe the original design was that the spirit/soul was not meant to be separated. It would be like seeing a man with a nice brown suit on. The suit is his personality. Looking at the man, we wouldn't say, "Look at that man *and* that brown suit." The suit and the man are one. The suit gives the man a certain personality.

This illustration fails because the suit can come off of the man, whereas the soul is stuck to the spirit. We know the man and the suit are separate, but we don't take them apart when we think about the man. That's how it was with Adam. His spirit wore a personality, his soul.

The soul is so special to God. Jesus once said to the multitudes "For what will it profit a man if he gains the whole world, and loses his own soul?" (Mark 8:36). The soul is comprised of the will, mind and emotions. The center of the soul, one's will, is the key to humanity. The soul allows man to freely love God. Within the soul is the power of choice. This is what distinguishes humans from a programmed robot who only does what God wants. The soul is also very important to God's enemy. The soul is the enemy's gateway to access and control.

Adam was made from God's breath and the earth's dirt; we see the soul coming into existence when those two were combined. He now is spirit/soul/body. We're separating the parts of Adam here into the three parts instead of two because we want to get an understanding of how humans were initially made.

As long as we are on this earth, the three parts are integrated. What goes on in our bodies affects our thinking and our feelings. What goes on in our emotions and mind often affects our bodies. There is a natural coming together of all of the parts. The only time it really is all separated again is at death and at that time, the soul and spirit separate from the body (James 2:26).

So humans were made as one in the beginning, but from separate parts. Fallen humanity is broken, separated more than originally designed but the parts still have some integration. But as broken as we might be, God's ultimate desire in redemption is to make us whole again.

In the beginning Adam was whole. Adam's spirit came from God. God's Spirit overshadowed Adam. God's intentions for mankind were that he would run his life based on that unique relationship. I believe the energizing force of Adam before sin was his spirit. Subsequently his will, mind and emotions and his body were under the subjection of man's spirit. Adam and Eve had a close relationship with God through their spirit. The first humans were dependent on God for their very life.

God did not intend that mankind would have knowledge of good and evil apart from their relationship with him. He did not want them to live their lives based on their thoughts, feelings or physical impulses. Their body and soul (thoughts/feelings) were to be ruled by their spirit. They were created spirit (living) souls and spiritual beings operate best when ruled by their spirits. Of course, with God's Spirit connected to man's spirit, this was the winning combination! God put the tree of life in the Garden of Eden for Adam and Eve to chose life.

Let me give you a personal illustration of how we can live our lives based on our souls shaped by past experiences. When I was growing up, I would go to my father to ask for money, say for a school trip. We were very poor. My Dad would get out his wallet, start looking in it and questioning me more about how much money I needed, what it was for, and then he would look back in the wallet with such a painful expression on his face.

Well, after a few minutes of that, I was ready to say, "Never mind. I think I'll just stay home that day." God used my father after I had gotten married to do some things to bring healing to me in that area, but I realized last year that some of my thinking toward God and money had been shaped by the experiences I've had with my father.

At times I see God hesitating, questioning me, looking into his wallet with a pained expression on his face. Sometimes if I have to wait, I tell him, "That's okay. I'll do without."

I am to respond to God in faith believing, but because of my past experiences, I struggle with believing God in the financial area. As I grow in the Word and walking in the Spirit, I can walk differently in this area. Faith is a function of the Spirit. Because I have the memory in my mind (soul) of finances with my father, my mind needs to be renewed with new experiences of God's faithfulness, God's ability and the plain old Word of God about God in this area.

The First Choice
God gave the first couple a free will to love and obey him from a position of conscious choice. He desired men and women of like mind with him, not robots. God had strictly forbidden Adam and Eve from eating of the tree of the knowledge of good and evil. This was the choice test. This was the point in which they could exercise their own free will. They were told the consequences if they chose to disobey: separation from God in death.

If they ate of the tree of life the first man and woman would have maintained their connection with an infinite God who knew all things. If they ate of the tree of the knowledge of good and evil, they would no longer have the Spirit of God overshadowing their own spirits.

Separated from God, decisions would have to be based on the principle of the knowledge of good and evil. They would be forced to live by their thoughts and feelings, by what their physical eyes and ears discerned. No longer having the benefit of the God of all wisdom and discernment as their covering, they would be subject to anything in the spirit arena.

Instead of being whole people with body and soul energized from their spirits, they would become broken (separated from God and separated from their own spirits) with the center of energy originating from a combination of the body and soul.

We know from God's proclamation when he created Adam that

the body was good. We know the soul was good. Everything God made was good. The physical body of humans has no intrinsic evil. All the functions of the body were designed by God and have good purpose, including our sex drive.

The result of eating of the tree of the knowledge of good and evil was that humanity moved away from a dependence upon God. The soul operates from another principle when it does not draw its strength from the spirit empowered by God's Spirit. That principle is death, not life. The soul operating under the principle of death is not a good source for our behavior. It is our flesh. That's why Paul says in Romans 7:18 that there was no good thing in his flesh.

The body and spirit did not become bad at the time of the fall. What happened is that confusion about God with the resulting shame, guilt, fear, hiding and blaming characterized Adam (Genesis 3:7-12). This was the result of sin, death, separation from God. The parts (spirit, body and soul) did not become evil but because the parts no longer operated from the source by which they were designed to operate, evil now had an inroad to humans (Genesis 3).

Because Adam messed up, all of us are born sinners, separated from God—confused with resulting shame, guilt, fear, hiding and blaming. We're incapable of pleasing God, falling short of his glory (Romans 3:23; 5:19).

We all start out energized by a combination of our bodies and souls and not our spirits and certainly not God's Spirit. As sinners after the pattern Adam gave us, our lives are also lived after the principle of the knowledge of good and evil. Though the parts themselves are not intrinsically evil, by the time we have acted, behaved and made decisions without God or have been acted upon by others who have acted, behaved and made ungodly decisions against us, much evil in our lives is the result.

After Adam, Jesus was an example of the next whole person to be born whose life reflected what it means to walk the earth the way it was originally designed. Jesus' body came from Mary. His body was like all of our bodies. His spirit came as a result of the placement of the seed from the Holy Spirit into Mary's womb. His soul, like every-one else's, was the result of his spirit coming into the physical body.

The difference with Jesus is that because God was his Father rather than an earthly father, Jesus lived his life by the principle of life rather than by the knowledge of good and evil. It tells us in 1 Corinthians 15:45, "The first man Adam became a living being. The last Adam became a life-giving spirit."

In Luke 2:52 the writer tells us that Jesus increased in wisdom and stature and in favor with God and man. Jesus operated his whole life as a whole person who depended on his connection with God. Like everyone else, he had a choice, but he chose to submit his will, his thoughts and emotions (soul) to his Father. He did and said nothing unless it came from his Father. Jesus came to do his Father's will. He sought his Father's plan all the time. We see him communicating with his Father all the time (Mark 1:35; John 4:34; 6:38).

God's Plan: Before the Foundation
Before the coming of time, God had a plan. God was confident he could convince mankind his way was better. God had a plan to give mankind another chance to choose the tree of life.

In the beginning, God provided his very own life to be in and upon Adam and Eve. They lost that protection when they sinned. At the point of independence from God, death occurred. Separated from the life of God, his outer covering of glory was lifted, and they be-came naked (Genesis 3:10).

God already had in place a plan to provide his very own life once again to be in and on us. This time that life was to come through his Son, Jesus Christ. God has given us the opportunity to regain the cov-ering Adam and Eve lost. If we partake of everything available to us through Jesus, we will have the ability to overcome the enemy not only in our lives, but also in the lives of our family, friends and neigh-bors. God provided everything necessary through the life and work of Jesus.

The Second Choice

Adam and Eve made their choice. They ate the fruit. Now we are paying the price. But we too have a choice. We can decide that we do not like the enemy's evil ways. We can choose the tree of life through Jesus Christ.

God is good and only desires the very best for all his children. African American women especially need to see how the deceiver has lied about the goodness of God. We have already gone behind the scenes and looked at how the enemy keeps us from the blessing of God in order to make God look bad.

We can now choose to whom we will direct our loyalty. It is essential for us as African American women to give our lives over to God unconditionally. As long as there are questions about God's goodness or even his ability to do the right thing lurking in our emotions, we will never give our lives to him in radical obedience.

Let's face it, the enemy has not gotten any stronger. God still has two-thirds of the angels on his side. Why don't we get out of the enemy's hands, away from his plans, and become tools in the hands of a mighty God?

In this period called time, the name of the game is the loyalty of mankind. Will mankind believe that God is a good God, has man's best interest at heart and is worthy to be trusted totally without conditions? Or is God evil, not to be trusted and unworthy to give our lives over to in an unconditional manner? Would we believe that the enemy has the best deal for us? Is God to be praised and the enemy damned or is God to be cursed and the enemy let off the hook?

Questions for Thought and Action

1. When did you make Jesus the Lord of your life?

2. Why do you think God gave humans a choice to obey him or not?

3. Explain how we now have a choice to eat from the tree of life.

4. Read Mark 1:35, John 4:34 and John 6:38. From these verses, what was most important to Jesus in doing what he did?

What are the two principles the author says we all need to live our lives by? How could these help you?

4. *Going deeper:* What does "we were all born sinners" mean? Support your answer from Scripture.

5. Describe how a past experience still has an affect on your present life. What would you like God to do to change that?

6. Take a moment now to meditate upon and pray aloud this prayer. (If you cannot pray it at this time, perhaps you will be able to at a later time.) "Father, I want to pattern my life after Jesus. Please help me to seek you daily concerning what I should do and how you would want me to live. Help me to listen to you before making decisions about the use of my time and energy. I want to be sensitized to hearing and knowing your voice."

9

Why Can't Black Men & Women Just Get Along?

• •

Lest Satan should take advantage of us;
for we are not ignorant of his devices.
(2 CORINTHIANS 2:11 NIV)

I give God the credit for keeping my husband and me together for over twenty-three years. My husband, Uwaifo Osaigbovo, is actually a very good man. The main problem is that he's a man, and you've probably already heard that "men are from Mars." Seriously, for all practical purposes, our marriage should not have lasted this long. Besides the male-female difference, my husband and I are as different as night and day in personality. The only personality trait we have in common is that we are both introverts. Add to that the fact that we have different values. He is the organized, left-brained, logical type, while I'm right brained and creative.

That would be enough differences to challenge anyone, but we are also from different cultures. He's from Nigeria, and I was born and raised in the southern United States. We have indeed had our share of misunderstandings and disappointments with each other. I think I know a little bit about two people trying to get along.

We are not supposed to be ignorant of Satan's devices. Many times we are. We've already looked at some facts about the enemy. Now that we have looked at the creation of humans, let's take a look at one of Satan's ways: his crooked plan to keep men and women divided.

We already stated the enemy was successful in his goal of getting humans to come away from a dependency on God and over to his side, severing the connection between mankind and God. Created as spirit/souls encased in an earth suit, humans need to be dependent upon a spiritual reality. Well, when the dependency on God was cut off, guess who it defaulted to? You're right, the negative spiritual reality, Satan, whom we have already identified as our real enemy.

We have seen that Satan is ultimately behind all of the chaos and evil in our cities and world. He is behind all oppression. His strategy is to keep everyone from knowing and operating in their God-ordained purposes and power. But did you know that Satan was behind the divisions between black men and women?

Division Is One of the Enemy's Ways
"If a kingdom is divided against itself, that kingdom cannot stand. And if a house is divided against itself, that house cannot stand" (Mark 3:24-25). Have you ever wondered why black men and women have so many problems getting along? Neither men nor women alone can solve the problems in our communities. We need to work together.

From the beginning of time, Satan's plan has been to destroy the unity existing between men and women. I think he has perfected his strategy in the black community. After sin entered the world, division became an issue. Before that the woman and man had worked together in coreigning over the earth. They were given dominion over the earth, to subdue it. They could have both done it together!

Togetherness: God's Original Plan
God is made up of three persons, the Father, the Son and the Holy

Spirit. When God decided to make humankind, the Bible tells us that God said "Let *us* make man in *our* image, after *our* likeness."

God made the first man, Adam singular. God made Adam the completion of mankind. The initial Adam was a unique blend of all traits and characteristics of both male and female. He was complete in himself, much as God the Trinity is complete in himself. But in being complete, Adam did not have one like himself to keep him company and to love. And by himself, he could not demonstrate the importance of unselfish living.

Maybe God looked at Adam and said to himself, "Two are better than one. . . . If one prevail against him, two shall withstand him; and a threefold cord is not quickly broken" (Ecclesiastes 4:9, 12 KJV).

Actually, what we have recorded for us in Genesis is that God said it was not good that man be alone (Genesis 2:18). So God took a rib from Adam's side and made another physical being. God planned: Together, they'll have dominion over all (Genesis 1:28).

God's purpose was togetherness. He knew united the first couple would stand. He also knew a house divided against itself would fall. God was aware one could chase a thousand, but two could put ten thousand to flight (Deuteronomy 32:30). There is multiplied power when a man and a woman are in harmony, united together against the enemy. When African American women learn to walk in God's ways, I believe we will win half of the battle between the sexes.

God separated Adam into two persons. God was the first to separate. In Genesis 2:21-23 we see God taking from Adam and making Eve. In the words of verse 23, "She was taken out of man."

The task at hand was to now walk in communion and togetherness in such a way that they would be able to effectively rule over the earth. Both members of the couple were important. As was previously mentioned, they were to remain connected to God in all they did. God wanted their life to be guided based on the life of God within, upon and with them. Together, connected to God, Adam and Eve would have been able to overcome the plot of the enemy.

However someone else was watching this whole chain of events.

The enemy was looking on and saying "Yeah, but divided, they'll fall" (Matthew 5:25). He then proceeded to successfully execute a fall. Satan approached the female part of the partnership and, by persuading her to act independently of her partner, he broke the connection between the man and the woman, putting the first rift between the two.

The bond between the first man and woman was powerful. One of the most powerful keys that a woman possesses is the power to influence. This key can be used by God. This key can also be used by the enemy.

Because of the power of influence, Adam chose to follow Eve. Instead of letting her be in her separation from God all by herself, Adam joined her with full knowledge of his actions. He chose to follow the woman he loved rather than the God he also loved. Eve's influence pulled Adam out of dependence upon God and into the enemy's hand.

Now Satan had them both.

When Eve and Adam ate of the tree of the knowledge of good and evil they bit into the nature of God's enemy. So instead of being rulers over everything on the earth, as God originally intended, they now become subjects to the rule of a new master.

Satan, the enemy of God, now has the right to control and use them as tools, hammers in his hands. This was the first transfer, from God's hand into the enemy's.

God intended the man and woman corule over the earth. He desired them to work together and subdue the enemy. His original plan was not totally forsaken. It was just put on the shelf until a later time.

Adam and Eve Face Consequences Too

The consequences for the relationship between Adam and Eve were forecast in the curse placed on them. God foretold mutual frustration and many difficulties maintaining togetherness.

God planned to be in complete control. When the first couple rebelled, he told them what was going to happen to both men and women without him in control of their lives. The curse of sin was God telling Adam and Eve what it was going to be like in their relationship with each other as a result of their independence from him.

It appears God's punishment for Adam was to let him experience exactly what God himself had experienced. God was the source from which Adam's spirit came. Even though instructed by God, Adam rebelled against God's command and took things into his own hands. Now Adam was going to get a taste of his own medicine. Adam was created first and was the source from which God built Eve. A result of sin was going to continue in the relationship between man and wife.

Adam would get a chance to experience rebellion, lack of submission, disobedience, disrespect and vying for control. According to Mark Littleton, the author of *Submission Is for Husbands, Too,* the word *desire* used in the phrase "your desire shall be for your husband" has the connotation of trying to dominate another.

For Eve's part, she was told she would experience domination as Adam maintained the rule over her. This was part of the curse. Adam would become not the servant-leader Jesus modeled but a domineering tyrant.

So we see the relationship between men and women did not have a good start after the fall. Satan has capitalized on this fact with many tricks of his own. He actually was the cause of the curse. He brought the curse of independence from God upon the entire human race.

I have a friend who once worked for a domestic violence shelter. Not that domestic violence does not exist among other ethnic groups, but the domestic violence shelters she was acquainted with were filled with mostly African American women. She believes domestic violence is at an all time high in the African American community.

Sometimes African American males are so frustrated with a society that continues to put him down. He feels helpless to go up against the system; so, many times, the sisters get the punch in the mouth he wanted to give the white boss.

Some of us have watched our mothers, or even our grandmothers, go through this kind of abuse. Even when we have not personally encountered it, we have made our inward vows, "I'm not going to take no mess." If a brother we're dealing with even looks like he might mess up, we're showing him the door.

Past hurts, past experiences of others, inward vows, protective shells, all of these keep the brothers and sisters divided.

As long as there is division between the sexes, God's original plan for humankind to defeat the enemy could never be fulfilled. Satan has tried to make sure togetherness would never reenter the earth's atmosphere. Satan's plan has been to put a permanent wedge between the sexes.

Through domination, strife, control, jealousy and contention, men and women and especially African American men and women have not been able to cooperate and neither have they been able to rule together effectively over the earth. Divided, they have not been able to properly bring up godly seed, or most importantly, destroy the enemy and his works.

Satan knew that divided, the first couple would fall. He wanted man and woman divided in the Garden of Eden, and he wants us as African American Christian men and women to stay divided in spite of what Jesus accomplished at Calvary.

My sisters, we don't have to stay divided. When we took a look at a woman's place, we saw that God's ultimate purpose of togetherness between the sexes had not come into reality for many of us, even as members of the body of Christ. But I still believe that his purpose will be accomplished as a result of the outpouring of God's Spirit on all flesh. As we pursue God, let's remember to pursue togetherness between the genders as well.

We thank God that the curse that was put on humankind as a result of the fall in the Garden of Eden can be overcome as we give our lives to Christ and as we walk and live by God's principles of *agape* love. Yes, with the true God in our midst, there is hope for relationships between black men and women to get better.

We've seen that it is possible to get connected back to God, through Jesus Christ. If you had not done it before beginning to read this book, I trust you are one who accepted God to be the new manager of your life. That's the best news available. Now at least you have a fighting chance to overcome your real enemy.

Without the life of Christ, we're doomed from the start; there is no hope. If you made that decision as a result of reading this book or if you renewed a prior commitment, please let someone who is a Christian know. If you have no one to share this with, share it with us. Information on how to contact us is found on page 237.

If you have never ever made that decision in your life, this book will just give you information, but you will not have the power to do much about what you read. But keep reading anyway. My prayer for you is that by the time you finish, you'll come to the conclusion that you want to give your all over to God.

Since many of us have at some point in time made the decision to give our lives to God, we may think we're home free now. But that is just not the case. Our enemy has a fierce resolve to keep us away from living in this world under God's spiritual laws.

Because of God's plans to use African American women as his chosen vessels, the devil has an extreme hatred for us and works overtime in our lives to especially keep us away from God and God's purposes. Part of Satan's plan to keep us distracted is to cause relationship problems.

Did you know that if we learn to follow God's ways, we do not have to succumb to Satan's plan of keeping division between black men and women?

Now that we are on God's side by accepting the life of Christ, the goal is to live by God's rules. God indeed provides a wall of protection for those who walk in obedience to him.

God delights in giving us wisdom to live in peaceful relationships. But spiritual laws are in operation. Spiritual laws govern the happenings of the world and our relationships with God and others.

God has given us a way to get to know him intimately through his Word. The Bible also contains the best relationship counsel available. You see, God made us and knows how we function. God desires to bless us. It is not God's design that we would struggle in our relationships all our lives. Consider the Scripture found below:

> Now it shall come to pass, if you diligently obey the voice of the LORD you God, to observe carefully all His commandments which I command you today, that the LORD you God will set you on high above all nations of the earth: And all these blessings shall come upon you, and overtake you, because you obey the voice of the LORD your God. (Deuteronomy 28:1-2)

Satan's whole plan is to trap us into operating on the negative side of the spiritual laws and thereby having God's favor removed. Satan's whole purpose in our life and community is to get us away from the blessings of God. Without the favor of God, we are open targets for the deceiver and all kinds of evil. When we don't operate under God's laws, we have trouble relating to each other.

Are African American Women Blocking God's Blessings?

All of Satan's evil is designed to get us away from the protecting hand of God and to get us to believe God does not have our best interests at heart. The things Satan does are designed to block the blessings of God. When we learn the rules of God's favor, we can learn the way that has been paved for us to live above the imaginations of the evil one.

My black Christian sisters, listen to God's heart. He desperately desires to get his goodness and blessing to us. He wants our relationships, whether with the other sisters in the church, our in-laws, our children or with our men, to reflect his glory.

He desires to answer our prayers. It's not a matter of twisting God's arm to get him to hear our prayers and give us his blessing. The issue is one of removing the blocks that keep the blessings from getting to us. The issue is one of learning how not to participate in activities that already have the curse of God on them. We must learn the way of the Spirit.

Derek Prince, in his book *Blessing or Curse: You Can Choose,* states the following:

> The operation of blessings and curses in our lives is not haphazard or unpredictable. On the contrary, both of them operate according to eternal, unchanging laws. It is to the Bible, once again, that we must look for a correct understanding of these laws.
>
> In Proverbs 26:2, Solomon establishes this principle with respect to curses: A curse without cause shall not alight. Behind every curse that comes upon us, there is a cause. If it seems that we are under a curse, we should seek to determine its cause.

A whole section of the above book is given to studying the biblical grounds for curses. From Scripture, it is pointed out how disrespect for parents, improper use of or disrespect for authority, oppressions against the weak including unborn babies, and the abuse and perversion of the sexual relationship will bring about God's curse.

These are all areas in which African Americans have struggles. Many of these struggles are rooted in slavery as we saw earlier. But the consequences of these struggles ruin our relationships with one another.

The enemy has been very clever. He has put together a well-designed plan to keep African American Christian women as recipients of the curse of sin and then divided and apart from our African American men.

God is our only help, but our enemy has lied to us about God. Satan has invested vast amounts of time and energy in keeping God's blessing away from African American Christian women. After he has achieved his objective, he then turns around and accuses God to us. In turn, we live with a hidden rift with God in our emotions. This rift continues to block God's best from getting to us. It also blocks us from receiving and practicing God's wisdom.

By recognizing the lies of the enemy, women of color can choose to discard them. Few have escaped the enemy's traps.

But no matter how successful the enemy has been, where sin abounds, grace abounds all the more (Romans 5:20). God is able to do exceedingly, abundantly more than we can ask or think according to his power that works in us (Ephesians 3:20)! God is able to reverse the curse in the relationships between black men and women.

I believe the first step in the fixing of the relationship between men and women is for women to come to a place in which our relationship with God is more important than a relationship with a man.

For many of us, a relationship with a human male is more important to us than our relationship with the Creator of the whole universe. This is true for sisters who are single and sisters who are married. It just looks different in each circumstance.

There is no way that we can put all of our energy into obtaining, maintaining, sustaining and retaining male/female relationships and still seek God with our all.

God desires us to have one goal in mind. Once all of our energy is focused on that one goal, God can direct all of the other good things he has in store for us. There is only one thing that is worthy of all of our energy. The psalmist had the right idea.

> One thing I have desired of the LORD,
> That will I seek:
> That I may dwell in the house of the LORD,
> All the days of my life,
> To behold the beauty of the LORD,
> And to inquire in His temple.
> For in the time of trouble
> He shall hide me in His pavilion;
> In the secret place of His tabernacle
> He shall hide me;
> He shall set me high upon a rock. (Psalm 27:4-5)

Some men have many problems in their attitudes toward women. We've mention how men do not value and treat God's chosen vessels properly. Some men abuse women. Some men use women. It's not good. A lot could be written to men to help them see things God's way; however I am not writing to the African American male. So my comments to them in this book would not achieve very much except to make you say "Amen. Tell it sister. I know that's right!" As you have probably noticed, that has not been my objective. My objective in this book is to help us make the changes we need to make.

So, I believe at least half of the problem in black male-female relationships are ones African American females can do something about.

I know some of your issues because I'm acquainted with my own. But I have some problems you don't have and vice versa. As we go through the next section, the healing section, I believe God will begin to speak to you to show you areas that he wants to heal and change in your life.

As you respond to God in the areas he brings to your attention, I believe you will begin to deal with some of the male-female issues that are under your control. I also believe as you get back under the blessings of God and increase your prayer power and ability, God will have access to begin to work on the African American men in your life.

For single sisters, I believe as God works in you, he will either wake up your Adam or be such a companion to you that you'll be content in singleness.

Let's review a few things that we have already established in this book that should help us in the area of male-female relationships.

First, men are not our enemy. Even the men who have hurt you were tools in our real enemy's hand. I am not saying this to let abusive men off the hook. I think everyone who allows Satan to use them for evil is still accountable for their actions. I am saying this because I believe it is possible for us to focus on the wrong foe and not get any understanding or help. So it is very important that we see who is behind the "hammers" in our lives.

Second, hurting people hurt people. Anyone who is so severely infected with spiritual germs that they would abuse another human being has been severely wounded. In this book we only talked about the wounded African American female, but the African American male has also suffered a lot of wounds.

Some wounds have occurred at the hand of the American society. There have been wounds suffered at the hand of some of us—by mothers, sisters and girlfriends. Again this is not to excuse evil behavior, but it is the truth. If we want things to change, we will need to look at how the healing balm of Jesus can be placed not only on our wounds but on the wounds of our men.

Most men are scared to admit they are hurting, but believe me, they are. It's behind much of their questionable behavior. We need to ask God for patience and mercy. We can be instruments of God's grace and comfort if we are willing.

Third, there is more power in prayer than we have yet experienced. Let us press into God to become the prayer warriors God desires to make us. Though I have not read it, a number of my friends have recommended *The Power of a Praying Wife* by Stormie Omartian. I am a believer in prayer; this will likely be a very good resource for those who want more help in this area.

Fourth, remember what Satan plans for evil, God can make good out of it. I often say it this way, "God is the greatest trash recycler that ever lived." No matter what we go through, God can heal us and use that experience to be of use to others. For that reason, we can take the chip off of our shoulder about the things that have happened to us.

Fifth, it may be necessary to leave an environment for safety reasons as David did after Saul sought to kill him. But even after separation, we do not have to give up. The purpose should be reconciliation and the establishment of a proper godly foundation (1 Corinthians 7:10-16).

Sixth, as believers, we need to learn to be responders instead of reacting to people and circumstances. God wants us to respond by the Word and the Spirit rather than our past experiences. We cannot expect God to come into our relationship and bring healing, peace and restoration if we are not committed to doing things God's way. Yes, that means we have to learn to overcome evil with good and pray for those who spitefully use us. It basically means we have to give up our neck jerking, hands on the hip, finger pointing, critical attitude and actions. Whether we literally do it, or do it in our minds; you know what I mean.

Questions for Thought and Action

1. Read 2 Corinthians 2:11 in your Bible, noting the surrounding context. Read it in at least one other version. Who wrote the passage? Who were the recipients of the passage? What insight does this give you regarding the verse.

2. *Going deeper:* What Scriptures affirm the power in unity?

Read Genesis chapters 1 and 2. God declared his creation good at the end of each day. What was the first thing God declared not good?

3. What special "woman power" is demonstrated when we see Adam following Eve in eating of the fruit of the tree he was forbidden to eat from?

4. Which of the following keep brothers and sisters divided? Explain your response. (a) past hurts (b) protective shells (c) inward vows (d) roots of bitterness

5. Explain how relationship problems can be used to keep us distracted.

6. Think about this question and answer very honestly: Is your relationship with God more important than a relationship or potential relationship with a human male?

7. If your answer is yes, how did you arrived at this point? If your answer is no, what might you need to change in order for you to come to that place?

8. What are some changes God is asking of us African American females that will make a difference in male-female relationships?

9. Take a moment now to meditate upon and pray aloud this prayer. (If you cannot pray it at this time, perhaps you will be able to at a later time.) "Father, I ask you to forgive me being an instrument of hurt in the life of an African American male. (If you remember specific incidents, admit those to God). I also forgive the African American males that have been used to hurt me. Pour your healing balm on hurting African American males and females. Tear down the walls that keep us apart. Amen."

10

balancing the scales

• •

For it is time for judgment to begin with the family of God;
and if it begins with us, what will the outcome be for those who
do not obey the gospel of God? (1 PETER 4:17 NIV)

fifty years ago, a black woman could not sit down next to a white man in a restaurant to eat a hamburger. Yet a few years ago, a black woman, Oprah Winfrey, was forced to take on wealthy beef ranchers in a lawsuit. She had done a show that put beef in a negative light. Because of her powerful influence in shaping people's thoughts, the ranchers could just see their profits fall, so they sued her for defamation, but Oprah won! Just think, here is a black woman who grew up in the South, was from a broken family, had experienced pain, struggles with weight, and yet today she holds that much power. We have come a long way!

Satan knows his fate is sealed when God takes hold of women and especially African American women and transfers them back into his hands! Satan has tried to stop us from getting back into God's hands. Satan has done it by lies, vicious lies about God, about us and about men. Satan has specifically targeted his attack at us. All of the actions of the enemy have been designed to circumvent the plan of God in the lives of African American Christian women.

But God has a plan that will circumvent all that Satan has done. We're in the midst of that plan right now. God is doing a new thing. He's ready to change things around.

Because of the pivotal role African American women play in homes, churches and communities, women who have been diverted from their purpose in Christ lead to a nation in crisis. We as a nation are under judgment.

Individuals have lost hope. Many are on the brink of despair. Our families need to be redeemed from strife and division. Our cities need to be rescued from the clutches of evil. Our nation needs healing. Change is needed in our nation.

God is able to heal our nation. There is nothing impossible with God. God's people have resources necessary to win the spiritual battles raging in our country. How do we get God's attention? How do we get an audience with God? And how do we get him to heal our land?

When something devastating such as an earthquake, a hurricane or a major fire happens, there's always been a lot of debate about whether that event constitutes the judgments of God. With every disaster some people are quick to say God is judging us as a nation because of the acts of sin we have committed. They point to the number of abortions, the rise in homosexuality and other things as the culprits.

Others say God had nothing to do with the disasters that happen. They tell us a loving God would never do those bad things. They assure us the devil is always behind those kind of events.

Both sides might have some truth. The fact of the matter is, as a righteous God, he abhors sin. As a loving God, he adores the sinner.

Look at it this way, when enough toxins build up in your body, you get sick. The disease is meant to let you know something is wrong, there's a need for cleansing, get some help, rest, get rid of some toxins. The disease will sometimes destroy healthy cells. But if the build-up of toxins continues in our bodies, more healthy cells will get destroyed and death may even occur.

Likewise, when there's a build-up of sin in the world, disease and disaster will also erupt. People who had nothing to do with the toxins (sins) will get hurt. But if the toxins continue to build up, even more people will get hurt and maybe the whole will self-destruct.

Satan's strategy is to cause sin to build up so that disaster will erupt. Satan wants destruction. He delights in seeing many people destroyed.

God is a God of judgment. When sins outweigh righteousness, judgment ensues. It's part of the natural cleansing, healing process required to maintain health. I don't think it really is a matter of whether or not God is judging America. It's a matter of how the scales of righteousness and sin are in balance. I believe the scales have been tilted toward sin a long time, but in his mercy God has held back major disaster. If we really knew the truth, we would be praising and magnifying God that he held it back this long.

God's laws of maintaining balance and health dictate the reason for disease and disaster. God's ultimate goal is health of the whole which can only be accomplished by reduction of toxins (sins).

The first way to avert judgment is for righteousness to outweigh unrighteousness. Whereas Satan is so intent on building up sin to bring destruction, God in his mercy is even more intent on alleviating judgment. In fact, God has given three different ways that judgment can be averted. As long as there is a remnant of righteous people, a nation is exalted (Proverbs 14:34). And it does not take a lot of righteous people to spare a nation.

Sodom and Gomorrah: Righteousness and Intercession

The first example is taken from the book of Genesis. In chapter 18 we see Abraham functioning as an intercessor for the cities of Sodom and Gomorrah. The sin of Sodom and Gomorrah was "very grievous," and because of that sin, the judgment God passed was destruction.

Abraham went to the Lord to intercede for the city. He actually bargained with God! "If there are fifty righteous people, will you spare the city? What about forty? Twenty? Ten?" As they continued to dialogue, God agreed to spare the city if only ten righteous people were found.

This account ends on a sad note. Sodom and Gomorrah were not spared. Ten righteous people were not found. However, God did spare four people by bringing them out of the city before the destruction. Some speculate that if Abraham had gone down to four, God might have even spared it upon his request.

That may be true. We know God will listen to his children. God wants to answer prayer. Many things are not done because God's people do not ask. "You lust and do not have. You murder and covet and cannot obtain. You fight and war. Yet you do not have because you do not ask" (James 4:2).

The second way to avert judgment is repentance. When people repent, God will repent of judgment. God always gives us plenty of warning when he is ready to mete out judgment. He sends his servants to tell us that our time is running out and encourages us to repent. Repentance is when people humble themselves, pray for mercy, seek God and turn from their sin (2 Chronicles 7:14). With repentance, the scales are tipped toward righteousness.

Nineveh: The Way of Repentance

The second place to look is in the book of Jonah. In Jonah 1:2 we see Jonah was to cry against wickedness and pronounce judgment against the city of Nineveh. He got sidetracked, but in Jonah 3:4, he cried out the following: "Yet forty days, and Nineveh shall be overthrown." Forty days came and went. No judgment came from God.

What happened? The people of Nineveh believed the word of God, fasted and repented. Actually, they followed the command of their King. He proclaimed a fast and told all of the people to be covered with sackcloth, cry mightily unto God, and turn away from their evil and violent ways.

Because the people repented (turned), God repented from the evil he had said he would do (Jonah 3:10).

Repentance is powerful. Repentance and intercession are unbeatable.

The third way to avert judgment is for someone who has an audience with God to ask God for mercy instead of judgment. God desires to give mercy so much, he actually seeks people (intercessors) who will ask him for mercy. This is often the plan that is put into action when people do not listen to the message of repentance from God's servants.

In Ezekiel 22:30 God is pleading for someone to ask him for mercy. The balance of sin had outweighed righteousness and God did not want to destroy the land so he wanted someone to stand in the gap. If someone had interceded for the land, God would have had a reason not to let judgment come. "So I sought for a man among them who would make a wall, and stand in the gap before Me on behalf of the land, that I should not destroy it; but I found no one."

We see this in the life of Moses. Twice he stood in the gap and God did not bring the destruction he was planning on bringing.

The first time is found in Exodus 32. When Moses had gone to meet with God and stayed a while, the children of Israel became impatient and asked Aaron to make a golden calf for them to worship. God was ready to consume everybody and start over with Moses.

Right away Moses prayed to God. Look at what he says:

Then Moses pleaded with the LORD, his God, and said: "LORD, why does Your wrath burn hot against Your people whom You have brought out of the land of Egypt with great power and with a mighty hand? Why should the Egyptians speak, and say, "He brought them out to harm them, to kill them in the mountains, and to consume them from the face of the earth'? Turn from Your fierce wrath, and relent from this harm to Your people. Remember Abraham, Isaac, and Israel, Your servants, to whom You swore by Your own self, and said to them, "I will multiply your descendants as the stars of heaven; and all this land that I have spoken of I give to your descendants, and they shall inherit it forever." So the LORD, relented from the harm which He said He would do to His people. (Exodus 32:11-14)

The second time is found in Numbers 12. Moses' sister Miriam complained about him. God became angry and took up for his servant Moses. Miriam was struck with leprosy. She would have died, but Moses interceded on her behalf. He asked the Lord to heal her and her life was spared (Numbers 12:13).

So you see intercession is powerful in averting judgment. We can increase righteousness, repent or ask God for mercy for those who have been wrong. All of these are means of balancing the scales toward averting judgment.

How Do the Cities in America Weigh In?

In the case of Nineveh, judgment was averted. The proper conditions were met. What would it be in the cases of Detroit or Chicago? How would Atlanta, New York, Los Angeles and San Francisco fare?

When God weighs these cities will he find more sin on the part of the unrighteous or more righteousness on the part of his people? What is the destiny of these cities? Is it possible for things to change?

One might say, "Well, we don't have a problem. I'm sure the city I live in will certainly find favor with God. I'm sure the enemy will not be allowed to bring destruction here. We have churches on every corner. We've got the religious people. Most of the people I know go to church."

"Wait a minute. Did you say religious people or righteous people?"

"Well, now I don't know. I'm not so sure. I can show you a lot of churches where people speak in tongues, or have Bible verses memorized or pack the folks in on Sunday. Certainly, these should count for something."

If we follow the set conditions, we have much hope for change. Solomon says in Proverbs 14:34 that righteousness exalts a nation, but sin is a reproach to any people. One of the words that describes the Hebrew word from which righteousness comes from is "cleansed."

The church is "America's only hope," to borrow a phrase from Dr.

Anthony Evans in his book of the same name. And prayer is the church's only hope. As the people of God turn to God in prayer, they will be cleansed so that the light will shine forth in the midst of the darkness.

Massive judgment has been averted in this nation because of the righteousness of the people of God and the prayers offered up in the past. But we would hate to wake up one morning and find out that the scales have been tipped. We have been spared much, but how much longer do we have before the sin outweighs the righteousness? From all indications there is not much time left.

No doubt God *has* blessed America. In spite of all of the wrongs we discussed, much good has come from this nation. But blessing time is running out. The enemy has increased evil faster than God's people have increased righteousness.

How would you, your family or church fare? Do you think increasing righteousness, repenting and asking God for mercy would be appropriate for yourself? This nation is made up of families. Families are made up of individuals. What can you do?

The Choice: Reducing Sin or Increasing Righteousness

In many cases Christians get upset with expressions of sins such as drug addiction, abortion or homosexuality. We all have probably gotten mail from well-meaning organizations whose focus is to reduce the number of people involved in these kinds of activities. But how much mail comes from organizations who want to increase the righteousness among those who have decided to follow Jesus?

If we look at the scales of sin and righteousness, there are two choices. We can either increase righteousness or we can decrease sin. If we maintain the same level of righteousness and somehow get sinners to stop sinning, the scales will tip to righteousness.

But decreasing sin must not be the only approach. It has some serious limitations. For one, we are trying to tell people to turn from their ways without the power of the Holy Spirit in their lives. That's unfair.

The other problem? Those who follow the "reducing sin" approach have little personal involvement in the lives of those against whom they protest. The perception on the outside goes something like this: "You don't really care about me as a person. All you see is what I do."

This is a true example from someone who worked at a crisis pregnancy center. "We were so focused on the clients that came in and making sure they carried their babies instead of aborting them. I believe we did help many people, but we did not look at our own self-righteous attitudes. I wonder if we could have made a bigger difference if we started out the day with a searchlight prayer for ourselves?"

How many of us good church folk have been guilty of judging those who come up in our churches with those revealing dresses. Often we're more concerned about her clothes than her soul.

Turning the Lights Back On Is a Better Way

It is much better to increase righteousness among the righteous. That will do two things. First, it will decrease sin among our own ranks. This will lower the effects of sin and also increase the effects of righteousness.

Second, it will bring light to those who are in darkness. People living in darkness are always drawn to the light. Our saltiness will make them thirsty, and many will come to the water to drink of the fountain of life, Jesus Christ.

Have you ever come home to a dark house, turned functioning lights on, and the darkness overcame the light? Darkness always disappears when lights are on. It will happen in our cities when Jesus begins to shine through God's people.

We have clear instructions from the Word of God how this happens. Again, prayer is the key. Prayer will tilt the scales and give us more time to reach the lost.

So far, everything has been pointing us back to prayer. We have said prayer is a key to the church's effectiveness and will avert certain judgment. Prayer is the key to saving our cities.

My African American sister, how do we make a "prayer move-ment" happen? Should we get more people to come to prayer servic-es? Should we call more national days of prayer?

That certainly would not hurt. But Scripture tells us the power of prayer is not found in numbers. If the number of people praying was the answer, we would have had the largest revival in the history of this country when over 300,000 people descended on Washington, D.C., to pray in the early 1990s.

Righteousness Is the Starting Place

Romans 6:13 says, "And do not present your members as instruments of unrighteousness to sin, but present yourselves to God as being alive from the dead, and your members as instruments of righteousness to God."

There are many sins of the body that need to be taken into ac-count. There are sins of the mind and tongue. They are the sins that got Israel into trouble and the same ones keeping us in trouble. Our families are being broken up by sins of the tongue. Churches are bro-ken by the destructive use of the tongue. Children's hearts are broken by the wrong use of the tongue.

Come on, Christian sisters, let us be honest and evaluate our lives under the microscope of the Word of God. In whose hand are you a tool? Are you used by God sometimes and by Satan at other times? A mixture indicates double-mindedness and instability (James 1:8). Are you a double agent?

In whose hand are you a tool?

God's Hand:

◆ thoughts/words of kindness, comfort, encouragement, exhorta-tion, forgiveness, mercy, blessing and acceptance seasoned with grace

◆ listens, prays, instructs, restores

◆ tries to help other change direction; gently confronts, rebukes and warns as needed, but only out of love and concern for the other per-son's well-being; done under the direction of the Holy Spirit, looking to herself; often accompanied by fasting

Satan's Hand:
◆ thoughts/words of criticism, condemnation, judgmentalism, bitterness, resentments, unforgiveness, anger, harshness, wrath and impatience
◆ uses silent treatment, withholds affection, withdraws or talks a lot without listening to others well, lashes out in anger, gossips or slanders
◆ prayerlessness or use of manipulative prayers
◆ always tries to correct or change others; corrects out of anger, harshly, without prayer and fasting and with an attitude of superiority

The prayer recipe in 2 Chronicles 7:14 says, "If my people, who are called by My name, will humble themselves, and pray, and seek My face, and turn from their wicked ways, then will I hear from heaven, and will forgive their sin and heal their land."

The responsibility of the healing of our land belongs to the people of God. It has four components. They are (1) humble yourself, (2) pray, (3) seek God's face and (4) turn from your wicked ways.

When people talk about this verse, they often refer to or emphasize just one or two ingredients in this four-part recipe. In fact, literature from a national prayer organization quoted this verse listing only three out of the four.

Most people know when it takes four ingredients to make a dish, trying to get by with just two or three does not work. If a cake recipe on the back of a Bisquick box calls for eggs, milk, sugar and Bisquick, using less than all four will not result in the cake. Eggs and milk make a scrambled egg mixture. The flour mixture and milk might make biscuits. Sugar, milk and eggs might make a protein drink. But none of these is the cake we wanted to make. In order to make the cake, we need to put in all four ingredients.

In order to heal our land, we need to follow the instructions given. The people of God need to humble ourselves. The people of God need to pray. The people of God need to seek God's face. The people of God need to turn from our wicked ways. If our land is not healed, then those responsible for the "cooking"—the people of God are at fault.

Can someone explain why Mr. and Mrs. My People are out of the kitchen, down the street telling Mr. and Mrs. Not My People what to do to bring healing to this land?

It's a little confusing. Perhaps we should get back into the kitchen. Maybe a few of us can get started on making this cake. Who knows? Others might join us!

Each one of these components listed in 2 Chronicles 7:14 requires action. It looks as if there might be a little work involved.

"You mean I just can't pray? I've got to humble myself too? What do you mean turn from my wicked ways? I don't have any wicked ways. Why, I read my Bible every day. I have read it all the way through twelve times. I go to church three times a week. I'm always seeking God. I am surely not like that man at the organ with "sugar in his tank" or those money hungry, skirt chasing preachers. And *please,* what about all those employers who don't want to give me a promotion because I'm black. Don't they know we got rights? They are the ones bringing our land to ruin! If we could just get them to stop all of their sinning, we would not be in the mess we're in. Where's the next protest?"

American Christianity is full of activity. There are plenty of petitions to sign, letters to write, demonstrations to attend and causes to support. There is a lot of criticism of the black church. Our mouths are definitely in action. If one is looking for action, look no further. There is merit to some of this kind of activity. But I fear much of it only serves to misdirect our focus of humbling ourselves, praying, seeking God's face and turning from our wicked ways. When we focus too much on what others should do, it makes us forget our own kitchen duties. It numbs us to our own responsibility. But of course, reducing sin can balance the scales. So I'm not against that part, as long as we put in the four ingredients we need to mix.

Prayer Will Increase Righteousness

If we pray the prayers of the prayer recipe, we will become the persons of prayer who actually have an audience with God. As we get more answers to prayer, we will pray more. As a result, we will begin to see more right living.

As African American women learn the prayers of the prayer recipe, God can teach us to possess the land of our families and our communities. We can be the vessels God will use to heal the broken hearts of many, bring deliverance, set at liberty them that are bruised and give sight to the blind. Yes, God can make us weapons of love and light to send us into enemy territory and bring freedom to many!

Let us accept our responsibility to increase righteousness. Let us stop looking to the government and others to bring change to our communities and this land. If we would lay our lives down in prayer, righteousness can be increased.

We could see change if we had a few more living righteous lives. We could see change everywhere if God's people followed the recipe of humbling, praying, seeking and turning.

It is easier to blame others for the ills of our society than to accept the truth about our own failures. It's a little humbling to admit we have wicked ways. Maybe we need to sing this song: "It's not the homosexual, it's not the crooked preacher or the crack dealer, but it's me O Lord, standing in the need of prayer . . ."

The next section of the book will explore the journey to wholeness. God has already initiated this process in many African American Christian women. Perhaps it has already begun in your life as well. It's a journey into the presence of God.

God's presence will reverse the enemy's work in our lives. His presence will give us back the ability to fulfill the original plan of destroying the works of the enemy and bring hope to our homes and communities.

Becoming a house of prayer instead of a den of thieves is a result of God's glory in our lives. I entreat you to sincerely pray the prayers listed in the next four chapters. The chapter on being humble looks at prayers that help us to cooperate with that ingredient. Each chapter takes an ingredient and does likewise.

These four ingredients are keys to God's purposes and our healing.

Before we get to pray the prayers that will bring change to our community, we need to pray the prayers that will bring healing to our wounded hearts.

Questions for Thought and Action

1. According to the chapter, what are the three ways to avert judgment?

2. Read Jonah 3:5-10. If God warned you ahead of time, would you be willing to fast for three days to avert disaster in your family or church? Name one past crisis you would have gladly fasted for three days to avert.

3. Read the account in Numbers 12:1-13. What would have been your prayer to the Lord on the behalf of someone who had just spoken against you?

4. *Going deeper:* Go over the list of tools. In whose hand are you a tool? Mark what is appropriate for you and see where you stand.

5. Without looking, list as many of the four ingredients to the prayer recipe as you can remember. Circle the ones you listed from memory. Now go back and add the ones you might have missed.

6. Why is it important for African American women to pray the prayers of the prayer recipe?

7. Luke 19:46 says, "My house is a house of prayer, but you have made it a den of thieves." Think about it. As Christians, our bodies are the temple of the Holy Spirit (1 Corinthians 6:19; 2 Corinthians 6:16). Which are you, a house of prayer or a den of thieves? Explain.

8. Take a moment now to meditate upon and pray aloud this prayer. (If you cannot pray it at this time, perhaps you will be able to at a later time.) "Father in heaven, I stand in prayer for my family. Father, forgive my parents and my grandparents for all the ways they did not follow you. Forgive me for all the ways I have not followed you. I ask you to have mercy on my family. I ask you to help us to turn from the behavior that displeases you. I ask you to remove judgment from our path. Amen."

part 4
the healing process

11

humble

◆ ◆ ◆ ◆ ◆ ◆ ◆ ◆ ◆ ◆ ◆ ◆ ◆ ◆ ◆ ◆ ◆ ◆ ◆ ◆

*Therefore humble yourselves under the mighty hand of God,
that He may exalt you in due time. (1 PETER 5:6)*

"Esohe! Come here right now and put this mayonnaise back up in the refrigerator. Why don't you ever put things back up? If I've told you once, I've told you a million times, put the food you use back up when you finish with it!"

"I didn't leave it out, Mommy."

"Oh, really. What? You think it walked out of the refrigerator by itself?"

Holy Spirit conviction: exaggeration—damaging a child's spirit—sarcasm—false accusation—excessive anger. "Lord, I was wrong. Forgive me."

"Listen, Esohe, I'm sorry I yelled at you this morning over the mayonnaise. After I thought about it, the Lord reminded me that I left it out. Forgive me for blaming you and fussing so. I was wrong."

It's humbling enough to admit it to ourselves when we are wrong.

To apologize to others is even more so. To apologize to your own children is not pleasant. Some people have the idea that children, students, employees (anyone under us) do not need an apology from us when we are wrong. I had the same idea until the first time God told me to apologize to my children for allowing my anger to get out of control. That was one way of dealing with the pride in my life.

"Well you go right ahead, sister apologize to your children if you want. But not me, I'm just not into that 'Let them see the real you stuff.' I'm not letting my kids see when I'm wrong. Mama told me that with your own kids, you're always right, even when you're wrong. If you show any weakness, they'll walk all over you."

I hear you, girlfriend. But don't put the book down, keep on reading.

When we realize how difficult it is to admit we are wrong to humans, it may indicate we have the same problem admitting our wrong to God. It's just so hard to humble ourselves before God and admit we are the ones at fault for a lot of things the enemy has done in our lives, our family members and even our cities.

The first step in humbling ourselves is confession, which means simply to agree with God. We need to agree with God where we have been wrong. Confession will lead to a change in our attitude of pride.

"But what do I confess? What have I done to contribute to the problems of our society?"

Many people honestly do not know what part they have played in society's ills. But we must at least agree to agree with God if he can show us.

The Importance of Admitting Our Sins

Sin gives an open invitation to evil spirits, the ones who work for our enemy, Satan, to work in our lives. It allows them to work in the circumstances of our lives. It gives them the legal right to block the blessings of God. Just as a parent does not desire for their children to be bullied, even if his child asked for it, God does not like Satan beating up on his children.

As Christians, we are covered by the blood of Jesus Christ. As long as we stay hidden in Christ, no matter our personal shortcomings, the enemy cannot get through to us. But when we step out of Christ and into sin, it is like painting ourselves with the florescent paint that attracts the attention of tormenting spirits.

If we confess/admit the sin, we get right back under the blood and are cleansed from all unrighteousness. We are really not any better than we were—the only difference is that we are not living out of our own abilities.

Hiding in Christ, we constantly depend upon the grace and power of God for righteous living. As we confess our faults, we are reminded that in our flesh is no good thing and that Christ is our righteousness (Romans 7:18; 1 Corinthians 1:30).

How Do We Know What to Confess?

The word of God says that we have not because we ask not (James 3:2). To find out if we have contributed to the problem, we need to ask God to open our eyes and show us. He said he would answer any prayer in line with his will. We know he desires us to have our eyes opened to truth (Luke 4:18; 2 Corinthians 4:4). The first prayer in our journey is to ask for help to see the things we need to confess.

David gives us an excellent example of this kind of prayer in Psalm 139:23-24. He says, "Search me, O God, and know my heart; try me, and know my anxieties; and see if there is any wicked way in me, and lead me in the way everlasting." We'll call this the searchlight prayer.

The searchlight prayer is desperately needed. It is an essential first prayer, truly a part of the humbling process. The psalmist tells us that if we regard iniquity in our hearts, God will not hear us (Psalm 66:18). The keystone of all prayer is for God to hear us. If he does not hear us, there is no possibility of a response.

The searchlight prayer is very important because we do not know our own hearts. The prophet in Jeremiah 17:9 says, "The heart is deceitful above all things, and desperately wicked; who can know it?" Only God knows our hearts (Psalm 44:21). David asks God to try his heart in Psalm 26:2. It is very possible to be deceived about our own righteousness, which to God is nothing but filthy rags (Isaiah 64:6).

Some Possible Surprises

Judgment begins in the household of faith. If we were to get the Judge's verdict, we might find we have been weighed in on the scales and found wanting. That has happened to me more than once.

Just recently I went to a free seminar titled "Detoxification for Weight Loss." As a little background, I had gained weight over the last six years. It began with my mother's death and increased ten to fifteen pounds with each of the three other deaths in my family. Hitting the age of forty with the normal slowing down of metabolism did not help. I knew I had a weight problem. I knew I didn't handle grief well. I knew I was not even practicing what I preached: "We should turn to God as the God of all comfort instead of food."

I just did not know how to get a grip on it; and once I had gained it, I wasn't taking it off. Well, I was finally getting a little motivation to do something about it because the excess weight was beginning to affect my physical health.

I wanted to see what they had to say at this seminar. Maybe they had some miracle cure so I wouldn't have to discipline myself with exercising or watching what I ate.

At the seminar they talked about the toxins that are in our body and how we needed to get to the root of things by getting the toxins cleansed out of our body, rather than always focusing on the symptoms the toxins bring.

While listening to the young lady talk about our physical bodies, I began to think about my spiritual life and my emotional life as well as the aches and pains I had been experiencing in my physical body. I knew that even the weight gain was a symptom of something deeper.

Now remember I'm the woman of faith and power, going all over the country telling women what God wants to do in and through us. I even had a seminar called "Becoming a House of Prayer" in which

I taught the searchlight prayer. I would say, "Everyone needs a spiritual check-up at least once a year. So even if you don't think you're sick, schedule your annual 'spiritual' anyway. You don't have to wait until you get symptoms." Wake up, Rebecca, maybe you were talking to yourself.

Tears came to my eyes in that detoxification seminar. So I took some of my own advice and sincerely cried out to the Lord to search my heart. I just prayed and asked the Lord to show me what was inside of me that was at the root of all my symptoms.

It wasn't even a week later and the test results came back: bitterness, resentments, anger. God showed me that deep down in my emotions, under what I consciously thought, I really did not like the way God appeared to have set it up with this husband/wife thing. It just was not fair. I was bitter and resentful toward the whole thing. Now mind you, I had taught on it, so I was not consciously aware of the bitterness deep inside. But when I saw symptoms and asked the Lord to expose the root, he was faithful.

I didn't like what he showed me. I wanted to argue that it just could not be true. But I had asked him to show me and he reminded me of that and what could I say? It was humbling. It was very embarrassing to know that all this stuff was in me, yet I had been teaching these things all along. I seriously tried to turn in my resignation from speaking or communicating to women.

Before the week was out, he showed me something else: rebelliousness.

That did it. "I'm just not fit to be used by you, Lord. I'm really messed up, more than I knew." Guess what I found out? He knew how messed up I was all along. It was no surprise to him. But you know, not even God can deal with what's in us as long as we don't know what's there.

And as far as God using me, I still can't figure that one out. But like I said early on in the preface of this book, "It's not about me." It really gives me more adoration and respect for his ability that he would use me as messed up as he knew me to be. And he didn't accept my resignation. He just told me I had to tell on myself and promised he would get all of the junk out and as a result be able to use me even more. Praise God!

It's important to get God's verdict on our lives and not someone else's or even our own word for it.

As you go to the Judge and ask him to search your heart, it is possible some of you who think you're on our way to heaven may find out that you've never really asked Jesus into your lives with your hearts. Oh, you've done so with your lips, but when he came to take you up on the invitation, you said, "Not now, not tonight." Some of you who think you are Christians are not.

A relationship, a habit or a self-appointed right to be bitter may have been the reason for the hesitation. After all we're human and we need a little affection, a little fun in life. We can't bring ourselves to give it all up.

God does not ask us to change before he comes in, but he does ask us to surrender all to him and allow him to make changes according to what he knows is best.

Others of you will get a not-so-good report like I did. I wish I could say that the above verdict on my life took place ten years ago. Actually, the first time I called in for a spiritual check-up due to experiencing some emotional pain did happen fourteen years ago. I didn't get good results then either. But what I just mentioned took place this year, a few months ago.

So you might find garbage in a basement closet like I did. Jesus has done a work of house cleaning in our lives and removed garbage out of the house. Why then would we rummage through the garbage later? We say, "It's so hard to let go of bitterness and resentment. Let's just keep it back in the closet. Who knows? I might need it someday." Look, the garbage is attracting flies. I thought you were committed to getting rid of the hooks the enemy had in your life. I assure you, you will not have any use for that garbage. Take my word for it, okay: I've tried to keep it too. It didn't work. *Let go of the anger, bitterness and resentment.* You'll be much lighter if you just let it go.

Rejoicing is in order for all who get a clean bill of spiritual health. We need healthy people. But even already healthy people will be able to do the work of God with new confidence. Voluntary exams are always better then being forced to seek attention.

How to Agree with the Findings

When individuals turn themselves in to the Chief Physician for a spiritual check-up and they get a surprise in their report, the same Physician will be able to fix it. We only need to be willing to admit (confess) when we get our test results.

> To some who were confident of their own righteousness and looked down on everybody else, Jesus told this parable: "Two men went up to the temple to pray, one a Pharisee and the other a tax collector. The Pharisee stood up and prayed about himself: 'God, I thank you that I am not like other men—robbers, evildoers, adulterers—or even like this tax collector. I fast twice a week and give a tenth of all I get.'
>
> "But the tax collector stood at a distance. He would not even look up to heaven, but beat his breast and said, 'God, have mercy on me, a sinner.'
>
> "I tell you that this man, rather than the other, went home justified before God. For everyone who exalts himself will be humbled, and he who humbles himself will be exalted." (Luke 18:9-14 NIV)

We all would do well to imitate the publican rather than the Pharisee in our prayers and attitudes. The publican asked for mercy for himself while the Pharisee was busy comparing himself with the sinner; he came out ahead in his own eyes. Sometimes our eyes are the only eyes in which we come out ahead. We can be so deceived about our own "good," it is pathetic. God's evaluation is essential.

Yes it can be humbling to find out some surprises that were buried, but humbling is the point of the first ingredient. However, that won't be the end. As the last part of verse 14 in the passage from Luke indicates, "For every one that exalts himself shall be abased, and every one that humbles himself will be exalted."

After God shows us our real heart, we agree he is correct. This is the prayer of confession. As already stated, confession simply means agreeing with God. We then ask him for mercy since his mercies are manifold (Nehemiah 9:19). We also know he is faithful and just to forgive us our sin and to cleanse us from all unrighteousness (1 John 1:9). By faith, we then ask him to clothe us in the righteousness of his Son (1 Corinthians 1:30; Philippians 3:9).

In humbling ourselves we may have to admit wrong to others, sometimes to those we have offended. Other times as we share our faults with members in the body of Christ in small fellowship groups, we will experience healing as others pray for us (James 5:16). Knowing our faults will also serve to keep us out of pride when God does have mercy on us and uses us. We'll know it was him, not us.

The day God revealed the true state of my heart a few months ago, I had just heard someone say that when we confess our sins to God, he forgives us according to 1 John 1:9, but when we confess our faults to one another and get prayer, we get healed as well. Well I wanted healing. So just everyone that called on the phone that day got my confession. If the mailman had stopped long enough, I would have told him too.

Yes, it was humbling to expose my dirty laundry to friends that day, but it was also healing. Yes, a lot of times I am talking to myself when God gives me a message, I think most of the time, that is the case. Even the times I spoke since then, God has had me expose my dirty laundry in public. Do I like it? Am I proud of these things? Do I like that I've gained weight? No, emphatically *no!* But it's the truth anyhow and God desires truth in our inward parts (Psalm 51:6).

I must also admit, that it's only at this third time of reading through and editing this manuscript that I've decided to include this confession. "I've got a reputation to maintain. Why would people listen to anything I say if they see all of my dirty laundry? Come on God, I have told on myself those times I spoke, isn't that enough? Maybe after I lose fifty pounds, I can talk about the weight thing. You know, there was a time when I had a weight problem. This was years ago . . ."

I still believe that no matter how messed up I am, how messed up you are, God can heal us. He even uses us in spite of our mess. Perhaps he prompts me to tell on myself so that you won't think that it's easy for me to say what I say because I don't have any problems. Maybe it's to destroy all misconceptions that I've got it together. Maybe it's to get more people to pray for me. (I like that one.) I don't know, but I do know God is still able to do more than I can ask or think and I'm going to keep on believing even if I don't see it all with my own eyes. He's still got work to do, but the outpouring of his Spirit will do the mighty work that needs to be done.

The Difficulty of These Prayers

We have discussed two types of prayers that are not often heard in most prayer meetings: the searchlight prayer and the prayer of confession. They are components of the humbling process.

How many prayer meetings have you been in where the only prayers prayed were the searchlight prayer and the prayer of confession? I bet not many. Oh yeah, we've got the praise and thanksgiving down. Some of us are even interceding for others. I would suggest that maybe we need to let some of those other prayers go and concentrate on these two for a while until God gets some breakthroughs in our heart.

There are many obstacles to these first two prayers. They look simple on paper, but in reality are very hard. Pride has a tremendous stronghold on most lives. It is very subtle. Pride keeps us from admitting there is anything wrong or makes excuses for obvious wrongs. We will have to call upon God often to be able to make it through the process of humility.

Denying, blaming or rationalizing are not compatible with humility. These are the things that we have to watch. Yep, I've tried the arguing approach too. "But God, that's not really me. You must have gotten my test results mixed up with someone else." It is almost certain all of us will try to get away with some of these defense mechanisms from time to time. But we must not tolerate them.

Fasting can help us to humble ourselves. David tells us in Psalm

35:13 that he humbled his soul with fasting. Fasting often accompanied confession of sin (1 Samuel 7:6; Nehemiah 9:1-2; Daniel 9:3).

The fast God chooses is spoken of in Isaiah 58:6-7. It is a fast to loose the bands of wickedness, to undo the heavy burdens, and to let the oppressed go free and break every yoke. Fasting is most effective if we are also concerned about what God is concerned about: sharing our food with the hungry, housing the homeless, clothing the naked, caring for our own and freeing the oppressed and bound. Let's not forget to turn from our wicked ways of putting our own yokes on people, pointing our finger in judgment and using our tongues to speak wickedly about others.

Fasting with the accompanying God-given actions is a must for those who would be burdened to pray for the healing of our land.

But first, we need to fast for ourselves. We are explicitly told by Joel to sanctify a fast and to call a solemn assembly (Joel 1:14; 2:12-15).

A person's health condition may preclude the advisability of fasting. If you have never fasted before, you should begin slowly. Seek a physician's counsel before embarking on any extended fast.

Although fasting can be done religiously and with pride by some (like the publican in Luke 18), that should not deter others from being obedient to God in this area. There are a lot of good resources on fasting. For more detailed information on the subject of fasting, the books *God's Chosen Fast* by Arthur Wallis and *Preparing for the Coming Revival* by Bill Bright are recommended.

Casting Our Cares on the Lord

We have looked at the aspect of humbling ourselves in three different ways: the searchlight prayer, the prayer of confession and fasting.

The next prayer is the casting prayer. In this prayer we give or cast all of our worries, cares, anxieties, concerns and burdens over to the Lord.

The Lord tell us in Matthew 11:30 that his yoke is easy and his burden is light. He also tells us in verses 28 and 29 to "come to Me, all you who labor and are heavy laden, and I will give you rest. Take My yoke upon you and learn from Me, for I am gentle and lowly in heart, and you will find rest for your souls."

The black community is plagued with serious health concerns that those in the medical profession blame on our emotional state. How many times have we heard someone say at a funeral she "worried herself to death." Worries and cares are an expenditure of much time and energy thinking about an issue. We fret about these issues over and over without coming to any conclusions and find ourselves going around in circles. According to Scripture, this is wrong. It signifies a lack of trust.

But it is unrealistic to suggest we should pretend nothing concerns us. In the casting prayer we give our concerns to the Lord, fully assured that he is able to care for us. We leave them there, and refuse to pick them back up by constantly trying to figure them out or falling back into old thinking habits.

What does casting our cares on God have to do with humility? Peter exhorts us in 1 Peter 5:7, "Cast all your care upon Him, for He cares for you." Just before that, Peter says in verses 5 and 6, "Be clothed with humility, for God resists the proud, but gives grace to the humble. Therefore humble yourself under the mighty hand of God, that he may exalt you in due time."

Ideally, we should give our concerns to the Lord and wait on the Lord to work them out. But we humans have the tendency to take back what we give the Lord. When we refuse to let God have our burdens, we're saying that we know more than he does. It is indeed one of the biggest evidences of pride in our lives.

Anytime we worry again about the thing we have committed to the Lord, we have taken it back. Now that does not mean that a thought can never cross our mind. That may happen. However, that's when we say to ourselves and anyone else, "That's not my problem anymore. Someone else is handling that." Then we let it go. If we need to, we go back to God and remind him that we chose to let that particular concern stay with him. But if God convicts us we have already taken something back, again we agree with his verdict of sin.

We thank him for his forgiveness and cleansing, ask him for help to leave it in his hands, and we recommit it to the Lord.

We may have to do this over and over again before we allow it to stay in his hands any length of time. Having to admit the inability to keep things in God's hands is humbling. Thank God that we can confess our sin as many times as it takes.

The Casting Prayer Brings Peace

When we truly cast all of our cares and concerns over to God, the result should be peace of mind. This prayer is dependent on a trust in God's faithfulness in the midst of adverse circumstances.

Paul states in Philippians 4:11-12 that he had learned to be content in whatever state he found himself. He knew both how to be abased (having nothing) and how to abound (having all things). God desires us to be unwavering in our confidence in him in spite of our circumstances.

In this life we will have trials. We will have to go through many fires and rivers, but God's Word promises he will be with us. "When you pass through the waters, I will be with you; and through the rivers, they shall not overflow you. When you walk through the fire, you shall not be burned, nor shall the flame scorch you" (Isaiah 43:2).

Scriptural Examples of Humility

The Scriptures give us many examples of those who knew their God and had learned to cast their cares on him. Most of our lives pale in comparison. The apostles in Acts 5 show us one example. In verses 40 and 41, after they were beaten, they left rejoicing that they were counted worthy to suffer shame for Jesus' name.

We see entirely different attitudes today. How many of us would do that? We would be going to the nearest lawyer to slap our persecutors with a lawsuit. It will be a glorious day when we are able by God's grace to jump for joy when people persecute or say all kinds of evil against us falsely for the sake of Jesus instead of always trying to defend ourselves.

There are a few things we can learn from the three Hebrew boys who were thrown in the fiery furnace. Daniel 3:17-18 quotes them as saying, "If that is the case, our God whom we serve is able to deliver us from the burning fiery furnace, and He will deliver us from your hand, O king. But if not, let it be known to you, O king, that we do not serve your gods, nor will we worship the golden image which you have set up."

The three young men were confident in the ability of their God to deliver. They also had an attitude of humility before God. In faith they declared God would deliver them, but they wanted the king to know that even if he would not deliver, they still would not serve his gods.

That was a humble attitude. They knew God could deliver them and believed he would deliver them, but refused to have the arrogance to demand that God deliver them. Much like the apostles in Acts 5, they were willing and ready to suffer for their faith even if it meant death.

The people referred to in both of the examples given above had one thing in common: they knew God. When we don't fully know God, we become fearful, wounded and frustrated when things go wrong. It is impossible to look at our circumstances correctly—that is, from God's point of view—without an in-depth knowledge of him. Daniel 11:32 says, "The people who know their God will display strength and take action" (NASB).

We are exhorted many times in Scripture to "humble ourselves." Many times we skip that requirement because it is painful to humble ourselves. We must remember that humbling ourselves is the first ingredient to the healing recipe. We can't jump over humble and just go to pray. Maybe that could be why our prayers are not being answered, we've skipped "humble."

Many African American Christians struggle with self-esteem issues. That's been a struggle of mine as well. I'm 5 feet, 10 inches tall. I've been this height since I was about twelve years old. I was taller than everybody in my sixth grade class, even all of the boys. (I was skinny back then though.) But I was ashamed of my height and developed poor posture because I didn't want to appear as tall as I was.

As missionaries my parents walked by faith. Their income was only that which others committed to give. My father did not have a congregation supporting him in the ministry. We lived below the poverty level. We wore secondhand clothes and shoes. So growing up, comparing what we owned with others it was not hard to realize most people had more than we did. I think being black in America you're always fighting feeling inferior. If it's not the material things, it's the education, or job advancements or just acceptance, whatever.

Sometimes because we feel inferior to others, we see that as humility. However inferiority and humility are far from being the same.

Humility knows God and knows one's identity in God. Humility knows one's strength and authority. Moses was said to be more humble than all men on the face of the earth (Numbers 12:3). Because of his relationship with God, he had no need to get upset or defend himself when others dissed him (Numbers 12:1-2). He knew God had his back. He could even pray that God would heal someone who talked about him (Numbers 12:13).

I believe that's the kind of authority and humility African American Christian women can walk in on a daily basis.

I have come a long way in seeing myself the way God sees me. Not that I don't still struggle at times, but I'm learning not to look at my worth based on what you have to say about me. I'm learning that comparing myself with others is not wise. There will always be those who have more than me, and also those who are more talented than me. But I am who I am and God loves and accepts me. Who am I to reject what God has accepted? You know what, I don't even accept your rejection. You can just keep it.

I've also learned to stop telling God I'm not good enough for his use. No, I don't have it all together. But God has given me grace, gifts and talents. He is the one who called me to himself. He is the one who asked me to serve him. When I argue with him, I'm just operating out of pride.

Our low self-esteem is really a pride issue because we do not see ourselves as God sees us. How dare we think of ourselves less than God made us. Are we higher than God to accept society's assessment rather than God's?

Paul tells us in Romans 12:3 not to think more highly of ourselves than we ought to think, but to think soberly as God has dealt to each one a measure of faith. Thinking soberly means not thinking lower of ourselves than we ought. Humility means seeing ourselves as God sees us, not too high and not too low. It means knowing that God has given us authority over the enemy, ability to love others and other gifts and abilities through his grace. We are who we are by the grace of God. There's no pride. There's no shame, just facts.

Three kinds of prayers are necessary to the humbling process: searchlight, casting and confession.

Maybe if we begin with the biblical ingredient of being humble, we'll find the crack houses and the abortion clinics closing because of a lack of customers. Similar things have happened before. Perhaps, if we would take the admonition to humble ourselves as seriously as we do our marching and petitioning, we could see more of God's agenda fulfilled.

Church-going African American Christian women, we can humble ourselves, admitting we are not really good representatives of Jesus' life and at the same time accept all that he has for us. That will put us in good position for the next prayers.

Questions for Thought and Action

1. Read 1 Peter 5:6 in your Bible, noting the surrounding context. Read it in at least one other version. Who wrote the passage? Who were the recipients of the passage? Write further insights regarding what humility is about.

Read 1 John 1:8-11. Why is hating a brother or sister stressed here?

2. How comfortable are you in apologizing to your children, students, employees, nieces, nephews? Have you ever done it? Would you ever do it? Explain.

3. Why is the searchlight prayer an important first prayer?

4. Why do you suppose the searchlight prayer and the prayer of confession are not heard more often in our church services?

5. What current cares do you have that you need to cast on the Lord?

6. *Going deeper:* Read Acts 5:17-42. Notice the response of the apostles in verses 40-42. What would have been your response to this situation?

7. Take a moment now to meditate upon and pray aloud this prayer. (If you cannot pray it at this time, perhaps you will be able to at a later time.) "Oh God, I really don't know my heart. I'm asking you to look into my heart and search me and show me any wrong motives or wrong thinking patterns. I agree to agree to whatever you show me. Help me to humble myself and accept whatever you reveal to me about my heart. Amen."

12

pray

◆ ◆

Is anyone among you suffering? Let him pray.
Is anyone cheerful? Let him sing psalms.
Is anyone among you sick? Let him call for the elders
of the church, and let them pray over him,
anointing him with oil in the name of the LORD.
And the prayer of faith will save the sick,
and the LORD shall raise him up.
And if he has committed sins, he will be forgiven him.
Confess your trespasses to one to another and pray one for another,
that you may be healed. The effectual, fervent prayer
of a righteous man avails much. (JAMES 5:13-16)

i have a friend whose husband credits his coming back to the Lord with her prayers. He had been active in serving God, loved the Lord and was a strong Christian for many years in their marriage. But some things had happened at church in which he was very hurt. He had really backslid and gone back to some of the lifestyle he had before becoming a Christian. He was still going to church. But his commitment level was a lot different. He wasn't doing things openly, but she would find tell-tell signs of places he had visited and things he was indulging in, things that were inconsistent with the Christian walk.

My friend didn't know what to do. She was very concerned about her husband. She prayed. She fasted. In fact her children would often join her in fasting. They didn't know details, but she would ask them to skip lunch and pray for their Dad. At night when he was asleep, she would put oil on him praying over him. (She found out later that many of those nights he wasn't asleep and knew what she was doing.) After he decided to come back to the Lord, he gave testimony to others in their church that "I'm back where I am with God today because of my wife's prayers."

The next ingredient in the recipe is prayer. Prayer is powerful, but there are a few things we want to say about prayer to help us tap into that power. After we have humbled ourselves, we are ready to bring our petitions to God. We have already been praying as we have gone to God to ask him to search us and have agreed with the things he has revealed to us. Now what petitions should we pray?

We should ask God for things clearly consistent with the promises of God. However, we should not just pull a verse out of the air and think it is sufficient. Even if we have a promise from Scripture, we need to be sure that the promise is appropriate for us. We must rightly divide the Word of God, and not just make it say what we want it to say (2 Timothy 2:15).

James 4:3 tells us that we ask and receive not because we ask amiss. That is, we ask with wrong motives in order to fulfill our own fleshly desires.

Is it really possible to go to God with the confidence he will answer our prayers? Imagine the power we would have for bringing change to our cities if God answered whatever we asked!

Many times Scripture promises to answer prayer. Let's look at some of those promises:

> And whatever you ask in My name, that I will do, that the Father may be glorified in the Son. If you ask anything in My name, I will do it. (John 14:13-14)
>
> If you abide in Me and My words abide in you, you will ask what you desire, and it shall be done for you. (John 15:7)

Beloved, if our heart does not condemn us, then have we confidence toward God. And whatever we ask we receive from Him, because we keep His commandments and do those things that are pleasing in His sight. And this is His commandment: that we should believe on the name of His Son Jesus Christ, and love one another, as He gave us commandment. (1 John 3:21-23)

Now this is the confidence that we have in Him, that, if we ask any thing according to His will, He hears us. And if we know that He hears us, whatever we ask, we know that we have the petitions that we have asked of Him. (1 John 5:14-15)

Yes, everything we ask can be answered. We should not be satisfied with "yes," "no" and "maybe" answers. The key is growing close to him so we pray the prayers he wants to answer "yes." That goal might take a long time to obtain, yet it should be our goal.

To be able to receive whatever we ask of God has nothing to do with God's ability to answer. It has to do with us. It happens when we have confidence toward God and ask according to his will. We have confidence toward God when we obey his commandments. We are told specifically which command is most important. It's the love command.

Love Is the Key to Answered Prayer

Sometimes we laugh about this "thing" that exists between African American women. You can be walking down the street and "sister girl" doesn't even know you, but if your hair is fixed better than hers or if you have a man on your arm and she doesn't, she'll give you that "I can't stand you" look. Unfortunately this "thing" also exists between sisters in the church. If one speaks or sings better than another there may be conflict and even feelings of hatred. This ought not to be.

If we are doing things pleasing to him, we love one another. As he is in us and as we are in him, we only ask those things that he wants in the first place. In this way, he answers all of our prayers.

If love is the key, what is love? God's love is different from the way we love. We love with conditions, but God puts no conditions on love.

(There are conditions to receive God's favor, friendship and blessings, but not his love because when we were yet sinners Christ died for us.) If we want to love the same way God loves, we have to love without conditions. That love is described in 1 Corinthians 13. This passage is a good reality check for us African American women in how we love our unsaved husbands, rebellious children and unruly neighbors.

> Love endures long and is patient and kind; love never is envious nor boils over with jealousy, is not boastful or vainglorious, does not display itself haughtily. It is not conceited (arrogant and inflated with pride); it is not rude (unmannerly) and does not insist on its own right or its own way, for it is not self-seeking; it is not touchy or fretful or resentful; it takes no account of the evil done to it [it pays no attention to a suffered wrong]. It does not rejoice at injustice and unrighteousness, but rejoices when right and truth prevail. Love bears up under anything and everything that comes, is ever ready to believe the best of every person, its hopes are fadeless under all circumstances and it endures everything [without weakening]. (1 Corinthians 4:4-7 Amplified Bible)

Love check up:

◆ Am I patient?
◆ Am I kind?
◆ Am I longsuffering?
◆ Do I rejoice when truth prevails?
◆ Do I believe the best of every person?
◆ Do I endure under everything?
◆ Do I rejoice when right prevails?
◆ Do I pay no attention when I suffer a wrong?
◆ Am I jealous?
◆ Am I boastful?
◆ Am I touchy?
◆ Am I resentful?
◆ Do I act haughtily?
◆ Do I insist on my way?
◆ Do I act rudely?

This unconditional love of God is already in us if we are Christians.

Why is God's love not seen through his people? God is love. His very character and life is unconditional love. The world desperately needs to see that love. This love dwells in the believer's spirit.

How is it that people can't see it? Each of us is like an individual "TV channel" to transmit God's love and presence to our world. Our signals can make for a cloudy or clear transmission.

The problem is not God's love. Our soul determines whether God's love will be clearly transmitted to others. The soul is the middleman. It stands between the spirit and the body. Bitterness, unforgiveness or fears tied up in our soul block God's love from flowing through us. The Holy Spirit has to overcome attitudes in our minds, desires and emotions to get through to our behavior and responses. What is in our spirit can then be demonstrated to the world.

Hurting people hurt people. It has really been a shock to me to find out that I have hurt people. I always considered myself as a kind person, going out of my way to treat people nice. (Okay, okay. I do realize when I'm on a mission from God to speak to his people, I tend to carry a sharp sword. People do tend to need band-aids after listening to me speak. Others say the band-aids are not enough, they need body casts.)

But I'm just talking on a general level. In relationships with Christian women, I have hurt others and have also had my share of hurts from others. It's inevitable. I remember a time, I just told the Lord, "Look, me and you is fine. But people hurt too much. I really don't want to be bothered with your people again. I don't want any relationships!" My patience and longsuffering were running thin. God showed me that if I ran away from relationships, I would be running away from the process he designed to build me up in his character.

Though the love is there in our spirit, there may be situations or people that make it hard for us to respond with God's unconditional love. Past experience may have instilled patterns of defensive emotional responses, negative thinking and selfish desires or expectations.

Essentially, what we are saying is we have to decide whether or not we want to take the risk of being transparent. Will we allow God's Word to change our negative thinking? Will we allow the Holy Spirit to comfort (heal) our emotional hurts? Will we forgive and forget unloving actions and attitudes we have experienced?

It's up to us to unclog the signals. We determine the clarity and clear transmission of our "channel" of blessing.

God's Spirit is ready to flow. He will help us put away the flesh and continue to fill us with his presence. He will make his love real to us.

God's Priority in Prayer

How many times in church or a prayer meeting has Sister So-and-So prayed for her lost son. Yes, God does want the lost son to come to Christ. But what he may want at this time more than the lost son found is character built in the mother who is praying. Sometimes when we pray, we want God to change the person or situation. That is not God's priority. God wants to change us more than he wants to change our situation. He's more interested in forming us into the image of his Son than he is in moving us out of our situations. He desires to bring all that is in our renewed Spirit into our soul, so that our behavior is godly.

The process of godly change should be worth more to us than anything else. It does not matter to God how much it costs in the natural realm to form the image of Christ in us.

Maybe we don't like to lose money, reputation or friends, but God does not mind if we lose these things to get his Son formed in us. The training may cost a lot to us, but it's nothing to God. He can replace anything it might cost. Whatever the devil means for evil, God can make it for good. That is one of the unique abilities of God.

When we get to know God better, some of these other things that we're seeking will begin to diminish in importance. This is when we start becoming a partner with God in prayer. Instead of always going to God with all the things we want, we begin to see the things that God wants to do in our lives and in the world around us. Then we go to God to ask his will and begin to see things happen.

Let's let the majority of our petitions to God be "Lord, change me. Lord, let your kingdom come into my life." For just a few minutes, let's just forget about the houses, boyfriends, cars, husbands, children, reputations, health and so on. Let's learn to seek him first, and he'll add all of these other things to us.

To Whom Do We Direct Our Petitions?

One last thing about petitions: I believe it is good to get into the habit of making most of our petitions to God the Father. Of course, in the time Jesus was on the earth, people came to him with their request. I don't think it is wrong to talk to Jesus in prayer, but in the model prayer of Matthew 6:9 in which Jesus instructed the disciples, he tells them to begin by saying "Our Father who art in heaven." Elsewhere in the Gospels, Jesus tells us to pray to the Father in his name (John 14:1).

I'm not saying that we can't make a request to Jesus or the Holy Spirit. It is all right to thank Jesus for what he accomplished on the cross. It is all right to acknowledge the help of the Holy Spirit in teaching and guiding us or even welcoming him in our midst. The Holy Spirit is present with us and it is all right to carry on a conversation with the Holy Spirit as we go about our day, but when we talk about entering the throne room with our petitions, the Scripture teaches that we should make these to the "Father." For whatever it's worth, maybe this little tip could help your prayer life.

When we begin to ask God to change us, we'll see changes in our circumstances and in our world. God can change us to manifest his unconditional love. That love is already within Christians. God brings it out by changing our emotional and thinking patterns. Love increases power in prayer. God's priority is his people.

Questions for Thought and Action

1. According to the chapter, there are some conditions for our prayers to be answered. What are these conditions?

(a) Ask for things that are clearly consistent _____ the _____ of _____.

(b) Ask with pure _____.

(c) Ask in _____'s _____.

(d) Abide in _____ and let his _____ _____ ____ _____.

(e) Keep his _____.

(f) Have _____ in God.

3. When have you ever noticed or experienced that "thing" between African American women which is described under "Love Is the Key to Answered Prayer"?

4. Do the "love check up." How did you come out?

☐ flying colors   ☐ Not too bad, just need a little work ☐ Not so good, need lots of work

5. Describe a time when you have really gotten fed up with the hurt you've experienced from other Christians.

6. What is God's priority in prayer?

7. How do we become a partner with God in prayer?

8. Take a moment now to meditate upon and pray aloud this prayer. (If you cannot pray it at this time, perhaps you will be able to at a later time.) " Father, change my thinking and emotional patterns so that your love can be clearly seen in my behavior. Amen."

9. *Going deeper:* What is another prayer that you know God would answer in your life?

13

seek

＊ ＊ ＊ ＊ ＊ ＊ ＊ ＊ ＊ ＊ ＊ ＊ ＊ ＊ ＊ ＊ ＊ ＊ ＊ ＊

But seek first the kingdom of God and His righteousness,
and all these things shall be added to you. (MATTHEW 6:33)

Again, the kingdom of heaven is like a merchant seeking beautiful pearls,
who, when he had found one pearl of great price,
went and sold all that he had and bought it. (MATTHEW 13:45-46)

god has blessed me with a couple of women who felt it laid on their hearts to keep me accountable with my health and weight struggles. I was walking with one this morning. She was telling me how God worked in her life concerning her weight. About eleven years ago, God began to deal with her. I was intrigued with how personal God was with her.

She started walking first. Then one day God told her, "Abbey, you love food more than you love me." She said she argued with God and told him no she didn't. He continued. "It's food you go to when you're happy, when you're sad and when you're angry. I want to be who you come to with all of that."

She had to admit that God was right. Food had become a substitute for what God wanted to be in her life.

God has dealt with me over the same conviction. He's shown me that I too use food as a source of comfort. That is idolatry in his eyes. We substitute a lot of false gods for the true and living God. What about you?

A lot of African American women love clothes. We could shop all day looking for the right outfit, the right hat. I mean we will spend the time, money and energy looking until we find. We have a goal. We are on a mission. We'll even skip lunch to find what we're looking for.

Do I need to talk about the energy some single women spend trying to find the right guy? Finding the right guy is constantly on their mind. Every decision is made with that goal in mind.

When we want something, we will usually find a way to get it, or waste a lot of time trying. How many of us are willing to seek God with the same intensity?

The things we substitute for God could be shopping, sex, smoking, drugs, church or a number of things we go to instead of going to God to get counsel, comfort, worth, value and other needs met.

Seeking God with our all means we are willing to give up everything in order to find the pearl of great price (Matthew 13:46). African American women, are we at this point? Sometimes when our lives seem so out of control, we work hard to maintain control, never allowing ourselves to get out of control again. If God is to be in control, we may need to give it up.

Seeking God indicates a willingness to put everything we cherish, depend upon and consider important aside and let God become most important in our lives. The prayer which pushes us toward that goal is the prayer of unconditional surrender to God. In it we tell God that nothing matters to us more than his Spirit controlling us.

In the prayer of unconditional surrender, we tell God the rule of his kingdom in our lives is more important to us than our careers, families, ministries, reputation, possessions, money or anything else we value. And we give him permission to test us on any of these points.

Let God Be God

We say we love and worship God, but often we are just in love with the traditions and structures of our religious systems. We don't mind being religious as long as we can do what we want to do. We don't mind going to church as long as we can go wherever we want the other days in the week. We can be religious as long as religion doesn't keep us from doing our own thing.

Christian sisters, if God was telling us to give up our women's days, our annual teas, our church fundraisers, and put them aside for more time in prayer or to serve in ministry by discipling some young women in the church—are we willing?

What we need more than anything else is to let God be God in our lives. He must be in complete control. Kingdom means reign. As we seek God's kingdom, let God have more and more control over our lives. Our security, worth, hope, expectation, confidence, attention, purpose and identity must be in God alone. We must turn to him only for comfort, wisdom, energy, resources and motivation.

Be warned: it is possible to make this commitment, forget it, and go on about our business, gradually losing the fervor we have for the Lord. The unconditional surrender prayer is not a "one time only" prayer. We will need to remind ourselves often and reaffirm to God that we still are holding on to our initial commitment.

For too long as a race, we have looked to the government, the lottery, our jobs and everything else to be the provider of our needs. We have looked to many things for comfort. We have looked to guns to be our protection; preachers and evangelists to be our teachers and guides. We have sought to find strength in organizations, sororities, church structures and legislation; worth and acceptance in positions and possessions. We need to repent of having all of these other gods before the one and only true God.

It says in Deuteronomy 5:7-9, "You shall have no other gods before Me. You shall not bow down to them, nor serve them. For I the LORD your God am a jealous God, visiting the iniquity of the fathers upon the children to the third and fourth generation of those who hate Me."

Deuteronomy 28:15, 20 tells us the consequences of not seeking:

"But it shall come to pass, if you do not obey the voice of the LORD your God. . . . The LORD will send on you cursing, confusion, and rebuke in all that you set you hand to do, until you are destroyed and until you perish quickly, because of the wickedness of your doings in which you have forsaken Me."

God is God. Nothing changes that. We spoke of his resume, but it did not include all that he is. There is no other god like him. There is no other god beside him. Everything else is false. Everything else is a front for the enemy of God.

God is the God of all comfort (2 Corinthians 1:3). He is all-powerful. God is our provider. God is wisdom and peace. He desires to function as our one and only God. He wants to determine our priorities in life.

In order to let God be God, we will have to be rid of all other false gods. If we know the false gods in our lives, we can voluntarily surrender them to God. However, many of us are not even aware of how many occupy our hearts. We do not have to worry. God can show us if we ask him. Even if we don't ask, he has ways of exposing them.

The Most Important Prayer

The unconditional surrender prayer may well be the most important prayer African American women can pray. If we do not pray this prayer, most other praying will be in vain.

The unconditional surrender prayer is essential to finding our way back into God's arms.

A lot of people treat God like a big granddad in the sky who will give everything they ask. But we need to get past that stage. As we grow, there are more and more responsibilities on our part. One thing we must do as we grow is to give God our all.

At a certain point of growth, God's response to us is based on how much of ourselves we give to him. Frankly he is not satisfied with less than everything. This is because he wants to give his everything to us. But if we hold back, he'll hold back. Then we're disappointed in him and hold back some more. He'll respond likewise. We should be drawing near to God, for as we draw near to God, he will draw near to us (James 4:8).

God wants unconditional surrender. He wants us to seek him first. He wants us to seek him with all of our heart, soul, mind and strength. He promises if we seek him with our all we will find him.

> Then shall you will call upon Me and go and pray to Me, and I will listen to you. And you will seek Me and find Me, when you search for Me with all your heart. And I will be found by you, says the LORD, and I will bring you back from your captivity. (Jeremiah 29:12-14)

The Attachments of Our Hearts

African American women, what would you miss the most if it was taken away from you? That is probably a good indicator of what your heart is grabbing on to, whether it is job security, food, marriage, a relationship, a career, a good reputation, nice possessions or a ministry. As long as we attach our heart to other things, we are selling ourselves short. We also do not allow God to fully work in our lives. God can do some great and powerful things in our lives, but we limit God by not giving him everything. That's why the searchlight prayer is so important. It can show us the things to which our hearts are attached.

If we don't pray the prayer of unconditional surrender and allow God to bring it to pass in our lives, our Christian lives will just continue to go in circles. We will never get full victory. We will never get to a place of intimacy with God.

We do not have to wait until we're certain God is number one before we pray this prayer. When we pray this prayer, God can then begin the lifetime process of making himself number one in our lives.

As God becomes first in our lives, other priorities will be shifted. The process of reducing the importance of other things in our lives is not pleasant, but is necessary in order for God to take his rightful place as God. This is the process of knowing God.

Most black women could write books about pain. It is as if there's a law: if it's black and female "beat it down till it can't stand up." Some of us feel like that so when we become a Christian we don't want to hear anything about *pain!* Yet the Bible talks about pain in a positive way and we need to understand the message.

The pain causes many people to either stand still or turn back. There is legitimate pain as God takes us from the realm of living out of the life of the carnal nature or the flesh to become people who live out of their spirits—identity with Christ. Galatians 5:16 tells us to walk in the Spirit and we won't fulfill the lust of the flesh. I define the flesh as the memory of old thought patterns, some of them strongholds of our mind that became entrenched in our brains when we were without Christ. Walking in the spirit instead of walking in flesh (what we are used to thinking, feeling and wanting based on our old life) can be painful.

It's much easier to react from old tapes and defense mechanism techniques than to do it God's way. Walking in the ways of God that have now been implanted into our brain on the basis of the new birth is like experiencing growing pains. We have a choice.

Charlotte, who is now in her fifties and a beautiful African American Christian woman talks about growing up thinking she was not anything special. She had short, can't-do-nothing-with-it hair, dark skin and big feet. She is still hearing that tape in her head. She came to Christ as an adult and is just now learning how to answer Satan's lie in that tape with God's truth.

The walk in the Spirit is nothing at all like the natural walk. In order for us to learn it, we are often taken through circumstances designed to force us to stay dependent upon God. These circumstances can cause temporary pain to our flesh.

Because of a waiting time between the promise of God and it's fulfillment, we often become impatient and run away from God into enemy territory. When we are deceived into thinking pain is to be avoided at all cost, we often refuse to grow up and thus continue to be a prey for the enemy.

Being Open with God
Part of unconditional surrender is being open with God. It's okay to

tell him where you really are. It's even okay to tell God we're not sure if it is really safe to give him unconditional surrender. We'll call this prayer the prayer of transparency. When we hurt, feel depressed or doubtful, we can tell God about it. God can handle our honesty.

Some Christians can't admit they are depressed. There are even teachings that insinuate that one should never say anything negative. I do believe we need to be careful what comes out of our mouths. There is power in the tongue to bring life or death (Proverbs 18:21). But so many African American women have taken that to the extreme. These women are not real. They don't want to say what they're going through because that would be making a "negative confession." Well, the Bible clearly says we are to share one another's burden. How can you share a burden if you can't say you have one? We need to come out from behind the masks and be real with each other.

Many times we pretend we are at peace when we are not. Sometimes we are angry with God, and will not admit it because we feel we have to keep up a front. If we are angry, worried or depressed, we should admit it to God and allow him to minister to us.

My Christian sisters, we cannot expect God to change our emotions if we refuse to acknowledge them. Sometimes we are so separated (broken) we do not even realize what is going on in our emotions.

Praising God in everything does not mean we live in denial. We can admit how we feel and still ask God to give us strength to praise him even though we do not feel like it. We then ask him to help our emotions follow along.

Practical Application of the Prayer of Transparency
Let's look at how this might work on a practical level. Let's say somebody in the church has made you angry. You may need to go to God and have a heart-to-heart talk. Let him know the person did really hurt you. You might say, "I'm angry about what Sister So-and-So did. It hurt. But I know that you are the God of all comfort. I need a touch

of your comfort to relieve my pain." You don't have to pretend you did not get hurt.

After our little talk with God, God may indicate he wants to help Sister So-and-So. He might tell you to go to her and let her know how you were offended. You're not trying to hurt her or to tell her off. It's purely out of a motive of love. Perhaps this is a pattern that has alienated her from others in the past (Matthew 18:15).

Getting to Know God

One of the really good ways to get to know God is to meditate on him and remind ourselves of who he is in spite of our circumstances. The enemy will have us believing if our circumstances are undesirable, God does not love us or he is not powerful. Even if it seems that God is not doing anything, we should still praise him for who he is and what he is. He is still God, regardless of our circumstances.

Most Christians really don't know God. We know a lot about him, and that's good. It's good to know about him. But we should really get to know his character. The mere fact we do not praise him more is an indication we do not know him well. The more you know God, the more you'll fall in love with him, and the more you will cease to worry about the trials and difficulties you encounter.

When we do that over and over, we expand our worship in prayer. After continuing in this way for some time God will reveal his character. This is how we learn to know God.

Another means of getting to know God is coming to God in silence, just waiting on him, just being near him. It's coming into God's presence without a request. You just want to get up in his lap and see if he has something to say to you. You'll be surprised at what God will say when he's given a chance to talk.

Most of the time, we're doing all the talking and he mostly can't get a word in edgewise. Don't be surprised if you hear him telling you of his love. Don't be surprised if he brings a little correction. You'll find yourself looking forward to hearing from him, more so than doing all the talking as you have been doing.

Having your Bible out and praying the Scriptures could be a help, but sometimes we don't need to say anything, just bask in his presence.

When we talk about praying, we are talking about coming into the presence of God Almighty, the Creator, the One who upholds the whole universe by the word of his power. We are talking about the one and only true God. We're speaking of one who owns and who made all things.

Isaiah 40:12 gives us some insight as to who God is: "Who has measured the waters in the hollow of His hand, measured heaven with the span, and calculated the dust of the earth in a measure? Weighed the mountains in scales and the hills in a balance?"

Remember God's resume? He's in control of everything. Nothing happens without his knowledge. He has all power, knows everything and is everywhere. When we go to God in prayer, we're going into the throne room of God to have an audience with the One who holds this world in his hand. When you really meditate on that, it is awesome!

Not many African American women will ever have the privilege of getting a personal audience with the President of the United States. But what if we did? Would we run in, blurt out a few requests and run back out?

"Definitely not," you say. But isn't that just what we sometimes do when we're in the presence of God Almighty? We don't always fully comprehend the awesome nature of that privilege, do we?

Praise Is Part of Seeking

You know what? A lot of people would have us believe their Bibles read, "Come into his presence with crying, whining and complaining."

The first words we need to utter when we come to God are words of thanksgiving and praise. In doing this we acknowledge the greatness of the One to whom we are talking. Let us look again to the Scriptures for insight into these prayers of worship.

Psalm 100:1-2 says, "Make a joyful noise unto the LORD, all ye lands. Serve the LORD with gladness: come before his presence with singing" (KJV). What is a joyful noise? It could be whatever you are comfortable with. Some people might be comfortable with shouting "Hallelujah." Others may be more comfortable with singing a song of praise. Either one is a joyful noise.

In the same psalm, verse 3 says, "Know ye that the LORD he is God: it is he that hath made us, and not we ourselves; we are his people, and the sheep of his pasture" (KJV). In this verse we are reminded of whom we are addressing. When we do not realize the Lord is God, sometimes we treat him as our servant. We did not make ourselves, he made us. We are his sheep, his people. He owns us, we do not own him. It is important that we remind ourselves of this. Otherwise, we come to him with attitudes of pride and arrogance.

Now we can enter his gates with thanksgiving and his courts with praise as indicated in verse 4. It is with an attitude of thankfulness that we are to bring our petitions and supplications to God.

Verse 4 tells us to "be thankful unto him, and bless his name." The word *bless* comes from a root that means to kneel. It has the idea of salute and praise. So when we bless his name, we acknowledge that we are beneath him in status. He is One to whom we bow. We come with an attitude of reverence. We offer praise and adoration to him.

It is also appropriate to physically kneel when we come to talk to him. Kneeling is a recommended posture. Again this helps the natural attitude of pride that is very much part of our flesh. Other postures are also scriptural.

In verse 5 we are again reminded of the character of God. This verse tells us "the LORD is good, his mercy is everlasting; and his truth endureth to all generations" (KJV). The Lord is good. Because his goodness may be blocked, our experience may not be in agreement with this fact. However let us not create additional blocks. Let us agree with God's Word that he is good. With time our circumstances will come in line with truth.

Thanksgiving and praise are really more for us than for God. Our

God is great, mighty, merciful and kind, and it is more than appropriate to praise and thank him for being who he is. We acknowledge truth with our lips even if our emotions do not feel up to it. We enter into his gates with thanksgiving and into his courts with praise. This can be done in song or spoken words, or both.

We can thank God not only for who he is but for what he has already done. For starters, we can thank God that Jesus paved the way for us to come into his presence. We can thank him for mercy and grace that allows us as humans to benefit from his goodness. We can thank him for the cleansing of sin and righteousness provided through his Son. There are so many things for which to be thankful and to give him praise.

Scriptural Examples

> Then the Levites of the children of the Kohathites and of the children of the Korahites stood up to praise the LORD God of Israel with voices loud and high. (2 Chronicles 20:19)

Did those Levites get a little carried away or what? Standing up and getting loud. My word. But they did not stop there. The next day when they were ready to go into battle, they appointed singers unto the Lord whose sole job was to sing and to praise the Lord.

Even the King Jehoshaphat seemed to go a little overboard by putting his face to the ground in worshiping the Lord according to 2 Chronicles 20:18. Does it really take all of that?

You can never praise God enough. God's strong presence is in the praise of his people (Psalm 22:3).

There is room for individuality in praise styles. A naturally quiet person may want to make a joyful noise by singing a song of thanksgiving.

Another person may want to shout, sing and then thank God for fifteen minutes before he brings his petitions. Others might want to lift their hands, clap and dance. All scriptural methods are valid. Most black churches are loud and active, but we should not judge the movement of God's Spirit by the amount of noise we make.

I came from a rather conservative church background. We didn't get into all of that emotional stuff. The first time I was in a meeting in which there were physical expressions of praise, I thought it was a little strange. But at the same time, God was showing me his greatness in my times with him in private. It became natural to express my love to him with my hands, lips, tears. Now, it's not such a chore to do it in public. I fear many are doing it in public who do not at all worship the Lord in private the same way.

The ultimate goal is to love God with all our heart, soul, mind and strength, and to love our neighbor as ourselves. Just as we cannot seek God only in part, we can't love God with a little bit; we have to give our all. That means that we have to take all the things that we are seeking or love and bring them under the love to God. God can help us to distribute our love everywhere else as long as he has it all.

But if we try to divide our love ourselves or love with conditions ("Lord, I'll love you if you will only do this"), it won't work. If we are honest with ourselves, we will see that we love a lot of things more than God.

Seeking God with our all involves an attitude of giving up everything in the prayer of unconditional surrender. We realize that the pearl of great price—having God control our lives—is worth our entire life.

As we must humbly ask God to teach us to walk in the spirit, we willingly surrender ideas of what it means to be a successful Christian and accept the possibility of learning all over again. As we get to know God, we open up our feelings to him in prayers of transparency.

We go to God with proper attitudes—attitudes of thanksgiving, praise, adoration in prayers of worship. We come to him with singing, joyfulness and gladness. We come to him in humility, bowing before him.

"It's not how high you jump and shout in church that counts, but it's how you walk once you've come down." Yes African American women, we can do the "holy dance" in church but how holy are our lives the rest of the week?

Cultivating a lifestyle of praise and thanksgiving is essential to one who desires to be used of God in prayer. And yes, it might even be necessary to get loud at times when we praise God. We may even get a little emotional and shed a few tears when we think of the goodness of God. For some, these methods of praise may not be customary. But change is in order if we want to turn our hearts toward God. Changing and turning is the subject of the next chapter.

Questions for Thought and Action

1. Can you identify one or more things you have substituted for God? Circle all that apply.

shopping	drugs	church	sex	food
friends	career	clothes	family	ministry
marriage	boyfriends	education	image	possessions

other_____   other_____   other_____

2. According to Deuteronomy 5:8-10 and 6:14-15, what are the consequences of having other gods (idols) before God?

3. Why is it important to admit to God our true emotional state?

4. Explain how you can praise God in everything and yet not live in denial of the problems you might have.

5. What is the difference between knowing God and knowing about God?

6. How do you feel when you are in a conversation with someone and have a difficult time getting a word in? How much can God identify with that feeling when you communicate with him in prayer?

7. *Going deeper:* When we come to God, what is the prayer attitude with which we should approach him? What Scripture texts tell us how to enter into God's presence?

8. Write out or pray aloud your own prayer of unconditional surrender.

14

turn

◆ ◆

That in reference to your former manner of life, you lay aside the old self,
which is being corrupted in accordance with the lusts of deceit,
and that you be renewed in the spirit of your mind,
and put on the new self, which in the likeness of God has been created
in righteousness and holiness of the truth.
(EPHESIANS 4:22-24 NASB)

I know a lady who has made some changes in her life. She has made a turn. When I first met her, she was very opinionated. From what she told me, she tended to say whatever came to her mind. She questioned God a lot. It was difficult for her to endure trials. She was impatient with her children.

I have seen the changes in her. Now, she is more willing to listen and say the things she feels God wants her to say. She is not so opinionated. She is more patient with her children. She's come a long way. She understands the ways of God better. Instead of being discouraged when things don't go the way she wants, she now boldly confronts the issues and has seen God work miraculously.

The changes are not natural for her, but she got tired of walking her old ways. She got tired of opening up the way for the enemy to continue to have a place in her life. She has sought help, studied the Word about the changes she needs to make and she is moving on up.

Sisters, there are many ways we need to turn away from. Some of the bedrock attitudes of African Americans are not godly. We need to be willing to put aside cultural tendencies if it is against the Word.

The last ingredient in our four-part recipe is to turn from our wicked ways. This is the action. It is most appropriate to talk about turning as we approach the end of our prayer journey. If you start at the very beginning of the prayer recipe, and put in the first three ingredients, turning is the logical conclusion. It is the action of putting off the old ways and putting on the ways of God.

What are the some wicked ways that you and I need to turn from? "But God, I know I'm not perfect, I know I have some problems, but wicked ways? That's a little strong, it sounds so evil. I'm a pretty good person. Come on, can't we just call it something more palatable?"

I've mentioned many wicked ways in my life that God has shown me were inconsistent with his ways. Turning from the wicked way of seeking the approval of people has not always been easy for me. I constantly struggle with wondering what others think of me. This is probably a struggle for other African American women as well.

One truth that has helped me is to realize that neither you, my friends nor anyone else will get to stand with me when I stand before the judgment seat of Christ (2 Corinthians 5:10) to endorse or vote against what I've done down here. It's just going to be me and the Lord. So if you're not going to be able to discredit what I've done, why should I worry what you think?

My focus needs to be on what God thinks of me and whether I'm obedient to him. I need to have the mind of Christ who only sought to do what God told him (John 5:19; 6:38). He not only did not seek the honor of people, but when they tried to give it to him, he refused to receive it (John 5:41). At each temptation to seek the approval of people, I have to consciously move in the opposite direction of my former pattern, according to the Word.

When I entertain bitterness or resentment toward my husband for whatever reason, instead of following the old pattern of clamming up and moving away, I have to, according to the Word, pray for him, talk to him and maybe even do something nice for him (Matthew 5:44; Luke 6:28; Romans 12:21). I may have to force myself to speak the truth in love (Ephesians 4:25).

Now I know some of you can't relate to this example. Clamming up, moving away—girl please! You're right there in brother man's face giving him a piece of your mind, maybe cussing him out. You're talking nonstop. You probably won't get the Scripture about speaking the truth in love. There are other Scriptures for you relating to the use of your mouth like Ephesians 4:29 and James 3:2-12.

> Know ye not, that so many of us as were baptized into Jesus Christ were baptized into his death? Therefore we are buried with him by baptism into death: that like as Christ was raised up from the dead by the glory of the Father, even so we also should walk in newness of life. For if we have been planted together in the likeness of his death, we shall be also in the likeness of his resurrection: Knowing this, that our old man is crucified with him, that the body of sin might be destroyed, that henceforth we should not serve sin. For he that is dead is freed from sin. (Romans 6:3-7 KJV)

This Scripture passage tells us our old nature died with Christ. It's not a sinful nature we have within us that we're struggling against, it's the flesh. Sometimes as an excuse we'll say, "Well you know, I still have my old sinful nature. I can't do any better." Wrong.

We've got the nature of God in us. The old nature has been crucified at the cross.

But we still have memories of old thought and emotional patterns. That's the flesh, the old self according to the opening Scripture in this chapter. That's what we are to put off. We are not to walk in the way of the old man or flesh. We are to walk in the way of the Spirit. We can choose to do better.

Walking in the spirit means utter dependence on the Lord. We need to realize that we can want this new life in Christ, but he has to do the work. Our responsibility is to crawl up on the surgeon's table and let him do the work. A friend told me that when she gets in the shower now or takes her bath she begins to pray, "Just as I am cleaning my outer skin, Lord, you do a cleaning on the inside of me. As I am scrubbing off outer dirt and odor you scrub out the inner. I'm helpless to walk this walk today without you. Fill every part of me with yourself. I'm totally dependent on you."

There is a big difference. Instead of an old nature we can't do anything about, we have attitudes, emotions and thinking patterns we can put off. When we choose the old instead of the new way deposited within our spirits, we continue to live fleshly lives. If we walk in the Spirit we do not fulfill the lust of the flesh (Galatians 5:16).

The war is a dual one. We are fighting both against our flesh (Galatians 5:16-21) and against evil spirits (Ephesians 6:12). Sometimes we must fight both at the same time. The flesh gives the hooks into our lives the enemy needs. Walking in the Spirit eliminates those hooks.

Satan's cohorts were instrumental in creating the hooks by arranging situations as early as childhood which left certain emotional and thought programs. These programs are the old patterns of hate, anger or insecurity which rise to the surface under the "right" circumstances.

Choosing the New Instead of the Old

The act of "turning" is the entrance into victorious living. It begins when we change our ways of thinking and reacting. By reacting in the flesh, we block the Holy Spirit from changing our soul.

Most Christians are taught to live the Christian life by the strength of their soul—that is, their mind, will and emotions. However, the soul is a part of the flesh if it does not draw its strength from the Spirit. God wants us to use our minds in studying his Word. He wants us to align our wills with his. And he can also use our emotions. Our mind, will and emotions are not bad, God just wants to align them with the character of the Spirit.

The way of the Spirit produces the fruit of the Spirit: love, joy, patience, peace, gentleness, goodness, meekness, temperance. God the Holy Spirit can begin a work of "turning" in our attitudes, behavior and reactions. But it is up to us to accept and use what has been provided. We simply must look to the Word of God and make the decision to change.

The struggle is one of choices. As we increase choosing the way of the Spirit, we strengthen new circuits in our minds which feed back into our behavior. The movement is upward; we are continually becoming more like Jesus.

The "Wicked Way" of Wrong Motivations

Some of our "wicked ways" seem right in our own eyes, but they are not the ways of God. He desires to remove even our "good" out of us if it is there by our own strength, on the shaky foundation of wrong motivations.

You might be praying or ministering publicly to impress others. You might be witnessing primarily to gain God's approval and acceptance. You might be trying to get your children to live right because you're embarrassed by their ungodly behavior. These are serious offenses to the cross of Christ.

Most of the time, we do not even consciously know we are operating from wrong or "mixed" motivations. We do not know our own hearts. God looks at the heart and not the outward behavior.

The light of God can expose the wrong motives. Paul, in Ephesians 5:11-14, speaks of the light reproving (exposing) the unfruitful works of darkness. If we are faithful to the searchlight prayer to ask God to show us our hearts, and the prayer of confession to admit what he shows us, now we have to be faithful to turn from the old ways.

Do you know that other people can help you see the blind spots in your life? All of us have blind spots. Though we ask God to search us or expose wrong motives, he may show us ourselves through other people. In fact, I've found out that God uses two kinds of people to let you see yourself: your friends and those who are very different from you. Sometimes you might see them as your enemies, but really they are just another kind of friend (Proverbs 27:6, 17).

Judgment: One of the Worst Offenses

What are the wicked ways of the people of God? One of them is the tendency to judge others by outward appearance. It happened even in the early church. Paul in 1 Corinthians 11:29-30 says that weakness, sickness and premature death occurred among the people of God because they "did not discern the Lord's body."

It appears taking the Lord's Supper unworthily has something to do with improperly respecting and recognizing all members of God's family. Today it could very well mean women, black, or poor members or even other ethnic groups that we are harboring ill feeling against. Come on, sisters, we know we have some prejudice problems too. It's not just them.

The folks whom God addresses in the book of James seemed to have a problem in this area as well (James 2:1-12). They were giving special time and attention to those who had money and ignoring the poor. They were the living embodiment of the verse in 1 Samuel 16:7: "Man looks at the outward appearance." But to continue that verse, "the Lord looks at the heart."

James tells us, "But if ye have respect to person, ye commit sin, and are convicted of the law as transgressors" (2:9 KJV). If we are going to be children of God, we must learn to judge as he judges . . . after the heart.

Isaiah 11:3 says that God will make Jesus "of quick understanding in the fear of the Lord," and that Jesus "shall not judge after the sight of his eyes, neither reprove after the hearing of his ears" (KJV). Jesus' ways are righteous.

When we judge someone or something by external characteristics, that is wicked. This includes judging someone by their size, their color, their gender, doctrinal beliefs, education, social status or any other criteria. We all have been guilty. African American women love to judge. We will size up another sister, looking her up and down and form an opinion about her within a few seconds.

This is a serious offense to God.

Judgmental and critical attitudes without a commitment to laying our lives down in prayer and a willingness to be used of God to come along beside another for restoration is a wicked way. We may be accurate in our assessment of how bad a person is, but God did not call us to assessment; he called us to be agents of change.

Instead of condemning based on appearance, we should ask the Lord to help us understand the person. Perhaps we'll find a broken heart there. If we are in a spiritual position to restore the person, that should be our next step (Galatians 6:1).

God called us to destroy the works of the enemy. He called us to heal the brokenhearted and give sight to the blind. As much as we might kid ourselves, we will not be able to effectively carry out our mission of being change agents as long as we allow attitudes of criticism and discrimination to remain in our hearts. Let us ask God to expose the places in our lives in which we are quick to judge. Let us turn from those ways.

How Should We Talk to God?
Do you talk with an attitude? Listen to yourself and other African American women. We have perfected the science of talking with an attitude. Unfortunately, often we come to God with this tone and attitude: "God! I don't know how long it's going to take you to do this simple thing. You really don't have too good a track record with me . . ." We're not actually saying this to him—we may say something like "Lord, you know I need a car," or "How long do I have to wait for a husband, Lord?"—but it is in our emotions and comes out in our attitude. We have to turn from coming to God in this manner. The discussion on praise and worship in the last chapter is the appropriate way to enter into God's presence.

Hebrews 4:6 speaks of a rest for the people of God. It says we must labor to enter that rest. As we learn to depend upon God, we will eventually enter into a rest. Instead of running back and forth, in this rest we abide in him.

Defeat will be certain if we think we have no choice but to be ruled by a sinful nature. Nothing can be done about a nature. But there is hope when we realize that the nature of God is within us and he will help us renew our minds. Romans 12:2 says, "Be transformed by the renewing of your mind, that you may prove what is that good and acceptable and perfect will of God."

The process of turning is painful. It means letting go of habits and attitudes with which you have grown to be comfortable. But what you gain is far more valuable. As we enter the final section of this book, the next chapter will show us how to cope with the pain as it describes "cooking in the oven."

Questions for Thought and Action

1. What are some ungodly ways that are part of your family traditions, your cultural heritage or just your own personality?

2. Read John 2:23-25; 5:34, 41-44. Why do you think Jesus did not commit himself to receive testimony or honor from people?

3. What's your pattern when you've been hurt by someone? (a) withdrawing from the person (b) getting in the person's face, arguing or fighting (c) some of both, depending on other factors

4. *Going deeper:* Write out Scriptures that could be helpful for turning from your old ways.

5. Why do you think most Christians try to change by drawing on their own strength, using mindpower, willpower or emotional fortitude, rather than letting the Spirit of God bring about the change?

6. Which of the following describes how you view sin? (a) The devil makes us do it (b) our old sinful nature is the culprit (c) though the devil may tempt us, we make a choice to do wrong

7. Do you agree or disagree that African American women also have problems with prejudice, criticisms and discrimination? Explain your answer.

8. Take a moment now to meditate upon and pray aloud this prayer. (If you cannot pray it at this time, perhaps you will be able to at a later time.) "Father, I don't want to continue to make excuses for

my actions. I know I can no longer use the devil as an excuse because you defeated him. I can't use the excuse of my old sinful nature because my old nature was crucified with Christ. Help me to take the responsibility of renewing my mind by your Word. I do believe you have given me all things that pertain to life and godliness. Help me to experience the knowledge of what you have made available to me."

Part 5
Let the Change Begin

15

baptism of fire

◆ ◆ ◆ ◆ ◆ ◆ ◆ ◆ ◆ ◆ ◆ ◆ ◆ ◆ ◆ ◆ ◆ ◆ ◆ ◆

John answered, saying to all,
"I indeed baptize you with water; but One mightier than I is coming,
whose sandal strap I am not worthy to loose.
He will baptize you with the Holy Spirit and with fire.
His winnowing fan is in His hand, and He will thoroughly clean out His
threshing floor, and gather the wheat into His barn;
but the chaff He will burn with unquenchable fire." (LUKE 3:16-17)

It was a dream, but it was very real. She was driving her car on a windy country road when everything suddenly went pitch black. There were no lights, not even in the car. Knowing that the road was full of curves, the driver decided to pull over and wait. But at that moment Jesus appeared and said, "Let me take over. I'll drive from here."

The Warning

My sisters, let me warn you, what we are going to say in this chapter may not be comfortable for you to hear. We have gone through each ingredient of the prayer recipe. We have looked at instructions on how to mix it all together. Now all we have to do is put it in the oven. The oven is a baptism of fire.

The baptism of fire is not comfortable. It is a place of intense heat.

It is designed to burn off anything that may hinder your growth in the kingdom.

God shakes those things out of us so that only what cannot be shaken is left. The fire of God then consumes the shaken things so we might receive his kingdom (Hebrews 12:26-29). Maybe your life is going through a shake and bake process. Rejoice, it might be from God. This chapter will help you come out intact, without smelling like smoke.

The Fire This Time . . .

The enemy is content as long as African American women walk in darkness. As you move through the prayer recipe and toward the light, he is going to be disturbed. He will be downright angry as he knows he is about to lose one of the greatest assets to his work: a Christian whose light does not shine.

He will increase his attacks against us. If in the past we were assigned three demons, he might well increase it to thirty demons. These demons will operate in the people and circumstances around us. Things will get so weird, at times we will contemplate giving up and returning to the mundane life of a "good American Christian."

The pressures will be great. The enemy will try to touch the most vulnerable areas of your life. For some it will be money or possessions. For others it might be health.

. . . Hits Us on the Inside Too

As your outside circumstances change, it is possible your mind, will and emotions—your flesh—will go haywire. Your mind will tell you it is not worth all the pain. Your emotions might experience discouragement, depression or rage as you try to cope in your own strength. You'll find things coming out you never knew were in you.

That is the enemy's objective. He will try to take away your peace, joy and unconditional love for God. As a result, you will be tempted to turn back. The stress may be that great.

Often the enemy will try to hit you in just the place where God wants to give you a ministry. If finances are a great struggle, it is possible God has a ministry of giving for you in his kingdom. If broken-ness has been your plight, God may desire to use you to bring wholeness to others.

The flesh does not want God to be in control. We find it more comfortable to walk after our own understanding than to acknowl-edge him in all our ways, letting him direct our paths. Life in the Spirit means self has to die. It's much easier to live a religious life than to live a life of the spirit of total dependency on God.

But we do not learn to live until we die (2 Corinthians 4:10-12).

The baptism of fire is a cleansing process. Our pride will be touched. We will have to face up to a lot of dirty laundry. It may be very embar-rassing as others see it. Buried junk in our lives will be brought to the surface so it can be skimmed off. We undergo reprogramming. We ex-perience major surgery in the spiritual realm. Surgery is painful.

But God is in the midst of the fire. He knows the very idols that we trust and is giving us the chance to let them go so that we might love and serve him with our all. He is answering the prayers of the prayer recipe. We have asked him to search us and cleanse us. We have sur-rendered all of our life to him and have said that we make him first and want nothing else to take his rightful place as Lord.

"The heart is deceitful above all things, and desperately wicked; who can know it? I, the LORD, search the heart, I test the mind (emo-tions), even to give every man according to his ways, and according to the fruit of his doings" (Jeremiah 17:9-10).

We do not know our own hearts. God shows us our hearts and gives us a chance to turn from our wicked ways. He gives us a chance to anchor our souls completely in him. As we let go of all of the other things that we are attached to, we will be free to be anchored in him.

But It Is for a Reason

Knowing that the testing of your faith produces patience. But let pa-tience have its perfect work, that you may be perfect and complete, lacking nothing. (James 1:3-4)

God is working in us a dependency on himself. Dependency upon God is precious. That's what God desperately wants to develop in us.

The goal of the adversary is to get us out from under the covering of God's favor. His purpose is to keep us at a distance from God and get us to think that God himself is actually the cause of the painful experiences we go through. If we are closer to the enemy than we are to God, we will actually blame God for our problems. When we do, we can actually fall into the enemy's snare.

But the pain is God's way of keeping us close to himself. It can serve many purposes. It can move us to come back underneath his protective wings. It can teach us about the goodness of God. It can spur us to spiritual growth.

God allows adverse circumstances and difficult people into our lives. The adverse circumstances purify our love for God. The difficult people help to purify our love for others. A sister-friend has a difficult relationship in her life that she is convinced God is using to bring her closer to himself.

I remember a time I was really worried about a loved one, was I ever praying and seeking God at that time. Did the situation change? Not really, but I changed. I heard from the Lord on the situation. Some of what I heard related to the person, some related to me.

Anybody else have a relationship that is a pain in the "you know what"? (Wow, I didn't expect so many "amens.")

These people and situations show us what is in our hearts. We may be able to put on a pretty good front most of the time, but we can't hide when God allows our lives to be "stirred up."

God has the same faith in us as he had in Job, that we will not curse him or love him any less. He's waiting for the time he can restore everything back to us double what it was before. But Satan is trying as hard as he can to get us to believe his lie that God does not love us and does not have our best interests at heart.

In the meantime, God is actually using the trials and tribulations to burn the flesh. God does not waste anything. Even what the enemy intends for evil, God can recycle for his glory.

Because of our broken hearts, a hard shell surrounds our lives. Chosen vessels have to be broken again, this time by God so his Spirit can be released through our lives.

The fire actually serves as training for God's army. Anyone who is aware they are in boot camp should not give up. Press on through to the glory, the presence of God. Trade in the pain for the glory.

For Many, the Fire Is Here

Fortunately many African American women do not have the fiery furnace to look forward to. They are in it now. Many of us have been undergoing boot camp for years and have not even understood what was going on.

Part of the reason it has lasted so long is because we have not cooperated with God. We have actually been angry with God. The boot camp experience is designed to come to an end. We will then be equipped to help others undergo this necessary cleansing.

Everybody will have to undergo a baptism of fire. There is really no option if we are going to be the people God wants. African American women who have lived in the fire can serve as guides to those who still have it ahead of them.

What to Do When "Going Through"

It is encouraging to see what God is doing in the lives of many women. However, it is discouraging to realize that some, in not understanding what God is doing, have become confused and angry, and have even resisted God's work. Proper understanding is essential.

Some of us are have more stubbornness and pride to be burned off than others. We cannot necessarily shorten the time required for God to complete his work, but we could prolong it. Admitting we have complained, murmured or been full of unbelief is the first step in coming out of a rut. Continuing all of the prayer steps—humility, commitment, seeking, turning—should keep us moving through.

The quickest way to get out of the fire is to learn to pray for and bless those—be they friend, foe, or family—who are causing us the pain in our furnace of fire. We can move into the realm of the Spirit by praying for the people Satan has used as hammers. For African American Christian women, this may mean whites and specific men.

Again, just as a reminder, our prayer for them is not for them to get out of our lives. Our prayer is for them to experience God's forgiveness, love, blessing and goodness. Our prayer is for their healing.

It is very likely the reason Saul of Tarsus (Acts 9) had such a dramatic conversion experience is because the kind of prayers mentioned above were prayed for him. When the new Christians began to murmur and complain about being persecuted, the apostles probably reminded them of the words of the Lord Jesus Christ that they should pray for their enemies. With that much prayer, the poor guy didn't have a chance. Our prayers will not only change us but can also open the door for God to deal with the person.

We must also pray the prayers previously discussed of confession, transparency and asking. The prayer of confession allows us to appropriate the provision of the cross and the blood of Jesus. We simply remind ourselves and agree with God that the blood of Jesus covers all of our sins and failures. Instead of providing our own inadequate covering, we allow him to cover us. The prayer of transparency allows us to be honest about our weakness, without blaming, denying, rationalizing or excusing ourselves. We ask God to change us. We also continue to cast our cares on him and renew our unconditional surrender as many times as needed.

The prayers of the prayer recipe are our keys to getting through this dark period. They force us to depend on God.

Another Prayer

As we progress on this journey into the reality of God's kingdom ruling in our lives and experience trials and difficulties, we are tempted to try to make it on our own. God will let us exhaust all of our own means until we are pushed into a corner with nowhere else to go.

We ask him to remove the source of pain. He tells us, "My grace is sufficient for you; for My strength is made perfect in weakness" (2 Corinthians 12:9).

Finally, we get the point and begin to call out to God with another prayer. This prayer was not discussed in the prayer recipe. But in a way, it is a combination of all of the prayers introduced. It is the prayer for grace. It is a simple request for help. Let's call it the SOS prayer.

When you send an SOS, the shorter the better. "Help" or "Help, Lord" is simple enough. Sometimes that is all we can get out of our mouths.

Our spiritual maturing will bring us into more of a dependency upon God. We'll find ourselves praying SOS prayers more, not less. The tricks and deceptions of the enemy will be so intensified that we'll need God more than ever.

How many times did we miss the opportunity that God was using to force us to lean on him and not to our own understanding?

No Time for Pain

Yes, my sisters, *more pain*. After the prayers, we submit ourselves to the fire, the trial of our faith. Let us submit ourselves under the mighty hand of God. God knows the "wicked ways" in each of us. The fire will burn it all—unless we resist or stay angry with God. The fire is intended to break the outward man so that the release of the Spirit might come through.

Sometimes as we go through the fire, we experience an intensified feeling of grief over all the pain buried in our hearts, pain we may have pushed down as a means of survival. Often we may find ourselves crying for no apparent reason. At this point it is vital we go to God for comfort as we let the tears flow.

If our pain has never experienced God's comfort, perhaps we have been turning to other temporary places for comfort. That's what I've done with food. You don't have to say amen, but you know it's the truth anyhow.

We are not promised getting rid of pain overnight, but there is relief! No matter how great the pain, we can get comfort from God. He is the God of all comfort. God can use his people as the tools to bring us comfort.

African American women, this is the time to stop fighting each other and begin to get to know one another and lean on each other. For many of us this will be a new thing. We have been hurt by each other and we are mistrustful. But we've got to come to the place where we can hurt, but hurt so good. I'm not saying go out and tell any and everybody your business, but we need to pray and ask God for some sisters we can trust and talk to, ones who will not spread our business around but will go to God in prayer on our behalf, encourage us and even tell us when we may be wrong.

Let others bear your burdens when you are going through (Galatians 6:2). There is so much God has for us through other members of the body of Christ. We often don't get the comfort God wants to give us because we do not want to be open and transparent with others. For me it's much easier to find the comfort in that cookie than to pick up the phone and tell a Christian friend that I'm hurting.

"Well, I don't want to shock them. They think I'm so strong. It would just mess them up for life if they were to find out that I'm not handling this too well. I've written two books. I've got to maintain the image of a strong black woman. Besides, I'm in the Lord's service. What would that do to the Lord's reputation if people knew I (his choice servant) am struggling? No, we've got to protect the Lord. That box of cookies will do." (Why are people looking at me so strange, can they see that box of cookies? I thought I threw the box away.)

How can you do the things God admonishes us to do with one another if we neglect true fellowship and the "one-another" things such as praying one for another, confessing our faults one to another, bearing one another's burdens, loving one another and all of the rest?

I believe God has given us each other in the body of Christ and has put into someone else everything that we all need for each other. But because we are so used to coming to church as spectators and not being the body parts for one another, we often don't find the help we need among the people of God.

I pray that we will get back to being what we need to be for each other, but in the meantime, some of us may have to go to Christian therapists to get the help we need.

Finally, let us even take joy in the wonderful work God is doing in our spiritual life. "My brethren (sisters), count it all joy when you fall into various trials" (James 1:2).

After the Fire

I'm so glad trouble don't last always. The fiery phase is temporary. It will not last forever. Our growth in grace and in the knowledge of God will continue as long as we live, but this major cleansing will not last beyond what is necessary. Even in the future, as God continues to expose and show us areas needing cleansing, it will not be as painful as this initial time.

So African American Christian sisters, don't be discouraged. Jesus died on Friday but Sunday is coming! We may go through the crucifixion but there is a resurrection day coming. I use to hear older women say, "It's just my burden to bear." However, the burden is to mold and develop you, not keep you bent over for life!

Also after the fire, we'll go out to rescue others because we have learned to operate under the full protection of God. After our fiery furnace, we will receive the enabling from God to defeat the devil in other's lives. In the meantime many others are still in need of comfort. In our own pain God was our comfort, and we comfort others with the comfort we received from God (2 Corinthians 1:4).

Many African American women who have been in the fires for years will find that as a result of submitting to the fires, they will be let out of the furnace. The end result will be similar to the three Hebrew boys in the book of Daniel. Not only were the ropes of bondage burned, but the boys were also joined by One who was like the Son of God (Daniel 3:25).

This is the hope to which we look forward. After our ropes are burned and the Spirit is released through the brokenness of the outer man, we, too, will experience sweet fellowship with Jesus Christ. Ironically, in spite of the experience of pain, we will begin to get a fresh understanding of God's love for us as he has finally removed all of the barriers to his goodness.

Many things come as a result of the fire. Yes, the pain, losses, disappointments from our sons and daughters, rejection and pain from our spouses, harassment from our bosses at work, even pain in our bodies is all very unpleasant. But if we only knew what we would receive as a result of it, we'd endure it singing praises to God. Purified precious gold comes out of the fire (1 Peter 1:9).

We will also learn the true meaning of praying "in Jesus' name." Praying in the name of Jesus is more than just tacking a phrase to the end of our prayers. It is praying with the righteousness and lifestyle of Jesus. It comes when God works his life out in our lives. It comes from passing through crises, experiences and rough terrain. To pray in his name is to live as he lived.

God's Presence

African American Christian women, here is the prize. The greatest gift at the end of our journey is to have the presence of God on our lives in tangible ways. The suffering will not compare to the glory that shall be. We won't have to wait until heaven to get a taste of the glory, God's presence in our life (Romans 8:17). That's the purpose for which God created us. Through the suffering, we can enter the glory of God. Are you shouting yet?

It is in his presence that we are his friends. It is there we have an open heaven, having the confidence to approach him.

If we allow patience to have her perfect work in us, we will come out on the other side of this fire. It is with much tribulation that we enter the kingdom (Acts 14:22). After the fiery tribulation, we enter God's reign, the rule of the Spirit. The kingdom brings righteousness, peace and joy (Romans 14:17).

The control of God's Holy Spirit brings the shedding abroad of the love of God in our hearts (Romans 5:2). When we experience and understand God's love for us, we will be free to love our Father with all of our hearts. We will be free to love our neighbors as ourselves.

People who are filled with the Spirit and Word are characterized by singing and making melody in their heart, singing to each other with songs and psalms and spiritual songs. Two verses that give us the proof of a Spirit-filled life are found in Ephesians 5:19 and Colossians 3:16. The true evidence of this Spirit/Word-filled life is singing when things are not going right, not when everything is going well (Acts 16). This is a way to know where you are in the process.

The purpose of spiritual maturity is to love beyond our human capacity. In this way, the Lord exchanges our strength for his strength. Sister, if we don't respond God's way, we prolong the trials and increase their severity. Women of color, haven't we suffered enough?

Just knowing a recipe does not produce a dish. We have seen what happens when we put the dish in the oven, the fiery furnace. We have looked at why the fire is so difficult and explored how to make it through.

There are many benefits to "going through"—God's kingdom rule in our life, evidence of the fruit of the Spirit, a new ability to help others, and the glory of God on our lives. Let's be encouraged to press on to the mark of the prize of the high calling of God in Christ Jesus. Let us go on through to the end. He has promised to be with us.

As we remember God has the ability to turn what is meant for evil against us for good, we will also see that God has a destiny for us and uses the suffering to prepare us for it. We will learn to cultivate a relationship with God while we are "going through." As we learn to genuinely forgive those the enemy has used to hurt us, we can use the anger to do battle against the real enemy!

We have discussed the prayers necessary to change African American women as individuals. As we change in our attitudes and behavior, we can help others change. Are you ready to reverse the curse?

Questions for Thought and Action

1. What experience have you gone through (or are currently in) that would be characteristic of what is termed "baptism of fire" in this chapter?

2. What kinds of things are accomplished in our lives from the pain, the adverse circumstances and the difficult people?

3. Read 2 Corinthians 12:7-10. What conclusion did the apostle Paul arrive at as a result of his difficult circumstance and his encounter with the Lord over it?

4. Explain how we receive comfort from God in our painful times.

5. Read the account of the three Hebrew boys in Daniel 3:8-27. What ropes do you want to be burned off of your life?

6. Read Romans 8:17. What does it mean that the suffering won't compare to the glory? Is that for heaven only? Explain your response.

7. *Going deeper:* Write down the possible destiny God has for you to minister to others based on your own personal painful experiences.

8. Take a moment now to meditate upon and pray aloud this prayer. (If you cannot pray it at this time, perhaps you will be able to at a later time.) "Father, I don't want to turn back when it's my turn to go through the firey furnace. Give me your grace in abundance so I might cease operating in my own strength and depend upon you. God, I surrender to your process."

16

reversing the curse

$\bullet \quad \bullet \quad \bullet \quad \bullet \quad \bullet \quad \bullet \quad \bullet \quad \bullet \quad \bullet \quad \bullet \quad \bullet \quad \bullet \quad \bullet \quad \bullet \quad \bullet \quad \bullet \quad \bullet \quad \bullet$

And you shall know the truth, and the truth shall make you free.
(JOHN 8:32)

god will reverse the curse on us as African American Christian women as we continue to follow the prayer recipe. It won't be easy to accept the things God exposes in our lives. Neither will it be easy to follow through in obedience to some things he wants us to do.

In the early part of my childhood, my father committed adultery several times against my mother. My mother was one of the sweetest women in the world and very passive. For years she put up with this treatment. I knew about my father's activities and harbored a lot of anger because I thought my mother should do something about it. When I was a teenager, it expressed itself in my rebellion. My mother taught me that sex before marriage was wrong, but I wouldn't listen. I was pregnant with my first child when I got married at a young age.

Not long into the marriage, I realized that I had married someone just like my father. He had other women and left me home with the baby. Well, I wasn't passive like my mother. I started going out too and got involved with another man (I'll call him Odis, but this is not his real name.) I really loved Odis, but I kept going back to my no-good husband. In the meantime, Odis married someone else. I finally divorced my husband and married someone else as well.

But Odis and I stayed in contact with each other. He eventually divorced his wife and we began to spend time together again. This time together produced a child. Finally, I told Odis I wanted to be faithful to my new husband. We stayed in touch for the sake of the child, but we no longer had an intimate relationship.

The moment I held my daughter (the one Odis had fathered) in my arms, I knew I didn't want her to experience all the pain in the relationships I had gone through, so I began to pray.

—Ermma

I attribute my making it to the altar as a virgin to my mother. When I was about three years old, she told me the story about the white wedding dress. She explained the significance of the white dress and how it was a privilege to wear one. She painted such a beautiful picture for me that from that point on I determined that it was what I wanted.

After I started school, if a boy peeked under my dress or wrote me a nasty note, I went straight home to tell Mama about it. I didn't want anything to keep me from my white wedding dress. My mother would drop whatever she had in her hand and would take me off into her room and listen to what I had to say, no matter how silly and insignificant. She wouldn't just inattentively listen, but she would actively ask questions, "Now what happened? And what did he say? And what did you say?" These little talks throughout grade school helped me to know that Mama was the place to come whenever I had problems or questions.

As I got older my mother would explain to me some of her own failures. Sometimes with tears in her eyes, she would tell me how she regretted the things she had done as a teenager and young adult. I know some parents fear sharing these kinds of experiences with their children, but for me it worked. I wanted no part of that kind of sexual action in my relationships. She was eighteen when everything started with her.

I was pressured in relationships. Especially in college. Everybody told me that I needed experience. I remember feeling like maybe I did. But I went home and talked to Mama about it first. She told me, "That's how everything started with me." As soon as Mama said that, I knew, pressure or no pressure, experience or not, I didn't want to go through the pain and hurt that my mother had experienced.

I used to explain to boys I went out with who pressured me sexually, "I want to wear a white dress when I get married. I do not want to have sex before marriage. And I want someone who understands that and respects it." If they kept pressuring me, I knew I needed to look elsewhere for the relationship I wanted.

When I finally met my husband, I still felt kind of bad about not having any experience. After we were engaged I explained to him very hesitantly, "Well I don't have any experience" as if that would make a big difference in our relationship. But he only said, "I'm a virgin too, and I don't have any experience either." I could hardly believe it. Not only had God kept me pure, but he had blessed me with a man who also had kept himself pure. And I got to wear the white wedding dress.

When we got married, the first couple of weeks took some time for us to adjust sexually. Things were slow going. Satan tried to run that game on both of us—"You should have gotten some experience." But after those first few weeks, this area of our marriage has been growing and developing beautifully. Mama was right; it was definitely worth the wait!

—Ermma's Daughter

I know this young lady. Her life is a blessing to many. She is raising godly daughters. Her mother put a stop to a generational curse. Yes, it is possible to reverse the curse. But it will take some humbling, some prayer, some seeking God's face and some turning from our wicked ways.

I will guarantee two things. (1) The dealings of the Spirit of God in our lives will be painful. No pain, no gain. (2) If we press through to freedom, our lives will be refreshed. The truth sets us free, but the truth also hurts.

The Antibiotic of Truth

In prior chapters we looked at some of the lies that Satan has put out against women and African Americans in particular. In order to reverse the effects of these lies, we have to give ourselves large doses of truth. Truth refutes lies. We must refuse the lies and accept the truth. It ultimately means accepting all Jesus did for us.

Truth exposes error. Light dispels darkness. Love erases hate and forgiveness swallows up bitterness. Jesus, who is not only truth but also love, light and forgiveness, is ready to set us free and send us forth to be a key to release others from their prisons.

There are several lies the enemy has tried to ingrain in the African American community. The first is that God does not love us as much because of our race. The truth is God loves all people equally. Acts 10:34 says, "God is no respecter of persons: but in every nation he that feareth him, and worketh righteousness, is accepted with him" (KJV).

Even when he chose to use the Jewish people for his own purposes, he made it clear to them that he did not pick them because they were more in number than others (Deuteronomy 7:7). Jesus also made it clear that his original intentions were to provide his truth to all nations (Matthew 28:19).

After the day of Pentecost, God proceeded to break down all barriers existing between Jews and other groups. He demonstrated his love to the black race by supernaturally reaching out to touch the Ethiopian eunuch in Acts 8. In that one act, he demonstrated that his provisions were not restricted to one group. A representative of the black race was one of the first God touched in the New Testament.

God continued to reach out to other groups until it was made abundantly clear his love was for everyone. John 3:16 says, "God so loved the world that He gave His only begotten Son, that whoever believes in Him should not perish but have everlasting life."

The second lie is that Africans and their descendants are under a permanent curse. Some would say that all who have black skin suffer because of the curse Noah put on his son Ham. Well that is just not true. First, Noah did not curse Ham. Take a look at that passage and see who was actually cursed. In Genesis 9:25 it was Ham's son Canaan who was cursed. The curse on the Canaanites was fulfilled when they were wiped out after the children of Israel came into the land of Canaan.

The third lie is blacks are inferior to other races. This is simply not true. In fact as a race, people of color from the continent of Africa were more advanced in the beginning of mankind beyond other races. Those with African blood had their turn at ruling the world.

More truth to counteract these lies can be found in a book by Dwight McKinsey, *Beyond Roots.*

The Real Destiny of African Americans

The fourth lie, that God cannot use African Americans, is really one of the biggest. In fact, one reason the enemy has fought us so hard is he knows the destiny of African Americans better than we know it.

I believe God wants to use those who have been rejected and oppressed by alcohol, drugs, immorality and prejudice such as African Americans, women, the young, poor, handicapped, foreign born and others to bring healing to this land. These will be trophies of God's grace and love.

Forgiveness: Key to Reversing the Curse

It is so important to release forgiveness to everyone the enemy has used against us. As we begin to forgive and release, we as African Americans can move to fulfill God's destinies, both in the spiritual and the natural arenas. God can do exceedingly abundantly more than we can ever ask or think.

We love others by forgiving them of their offenses against us. We can obey God by following Matthew 5:44, which says, "Love your enemies, bless those who curse you, do good to those who hate you, and pray for those who spitefully use you and persecute you." If we refuse to obey this, we give the enemy the right to continue his torment upon us.

We disobey when we harbor bitterness and unforgiveness, and thereby experience God's curse and not his blessing. To reemphasize, when we speak evil of someone, we curse them. When we speak well of someone, we bless them. When evil is spoken about us as a people, we need to bless instead of curse.

How can we speak well of others when they do such terrible things against us? We do it because God first forgave us. We do it because to do anything less will take us out of the place of favor with God. Nothing is worth that (Matthew 18:21-35). We do it because we want to reverse the curse on our lives, our families and our communities.

Hattie was in a domestic abuse situation with an alcoholic husband. She cried out to the Lord in her pain and confusion, which resulted in a closer walk with the Lord and in time a ministry to other women who are hurting. Even though her husband eventually left her for another woman, once Hattie had worked through her pain and confusion, she was prompted of the Lord to humble herself and go to her former husband and ask his forgiveness for her part of the bad marriage.

When we understand God's plans and purposes for our lives and how the things we have encountered are a part of his plan for us, we can forgive those we have been blaming for our difficult life.

The way to reverse a curse is the way of the Spirit. The way to continue a curse is to react in the flesh. We're talking about radical obedience to God, because our community needs radical surgery. The question is, do we want to inherit a blessing for our homes and communities or continue in curses?

In 1 Peter 3:9, the writer clearly tells us how we can inherit the blessing. It says "not returning evil for evil or reviling for reviling, but on the contrary blessing, knowing that you were called to this, that you may inherit a blessing." That's it right there. In order to inherit the blessings of God, we have to bless others who don't bless us. Paul did it and he was feared by the demons. When he was reviled, he blessed (1 Corinthians 4:12).

God wants to put the blessings of Abraham on us (Galatians 3:14). They don't come automatically, not just as a result of being a Christian. They come as the result of radical obedience. They come as a result of living the lifestyle of the Spirit of God. In case we need one more verse to convince us, look at Romans 12:14: "Bless those who persecute you; bless and do not curse."

We have to bless the men who have hurt us, our children who have caused us pain and whites who have done injustices to us. We do it because we want to receive God's blessings. This may be extremely difficult. People with broken hearts do not bless others easily. However before we get really hot under the collar, let us just remember God does not ask us to do anything that he will not give us the strength to do. God will perfect his strength in our weakness. God will enable us to do this (2 Corinthians 12:9).

African American women may say, "Yeah, but society's attitudes toward us will not change. Why should we have to do all the forgiving?" One can understand how many may feel this way. African American women have had many negative experiences. But we have to consider who wants things to remain the same. That is not God's plan. God has some new things on his mind. His plan is to turn things around. He can start with African American women.

In order to cooperate with God, we must choose not to cooperate with Satan. Satan is the one who has worked in our lives to bring an entanglement of destruction in our community. He is the one who hates women with a vengeance. He is the only one who wants to see us continue under the curse. We cooperate with him when we refuse to bless others.

African American women are in a unique position to be used of God to avert the increasing judgment on this nation. Praying African American women can use the power of God to stop many of the cycles of division. While being healed of the brokenness of our own heart, perhaps we can be lights to rescue others from the enemy's tactics they have erroneously followed.

We have the power to forgive all who have offended us in the past and those who continue to offend us today. We have to exercise that power. Our very lives and those of future generations depend upon it.

The Cost of Radical Obedience

It will cost us everything we have. It will cost us all of our false gods. It will be extremely uncomfortable.

Much of the pain we are going through right now could be used to thrust us into the kingdom of God. It is there, in the presence of God, that we have fullness of joy. It is there that we have divine protection. If we really understood how good it is living the ways of God, we would rather have the temporary pain of entering that realm than the constant pain of living by the enemy's rules.

God is our friend, not our enemy. We cannot afford to cooperate with Satan in any way. We will have to give ourselves over to radical obedience to God. We have to jump over to his side without reservation. It may be inconvenient and uncomfortable, but our community has lived enough with the enemy's plan. We need to see what God has to offer. We can't get God's best trying to straddle the fence.

The Bondage of Unforgiveness

God refuses to judge people we insist on judging. He is a fair God. It's not fair to have two judges. If we would release others into the hands of God, he'll do a lot better job of dealing with their wrong. And we'll be released of the burden as well.

Our unforgiveness is similar to bringing home a thief who stole our car in order to punish him. Now that we've got him locked up in our spare bedroom, we have to feed, guard and take care of him. We can't use the room anymore. We can't go out and have fun without worrying if he'll get away. That's a heavy responsibility.

However if we would just turn him over to the proper authorities, they can take care of all of that. Justice will be rendered, but not at our expense. God will not only take care of the thief but will also give us back our car and more.

God has many ways of making up for pain. In the example of Job in the Bible, God restored to him double what was taken. The latter part of Joseph's life made up for the first part. God can make up for years of pain women have suffered. God can make up for pain African Americans have suffered. God can show African American women how to reverse the damage let loose in this earth by the first disobedience of Adam and Eve as we learn to eat from the tree of life—Jesus Christ.

God knows how to bring about equity and justice. We have to let God be God. We have to stop looking to our own strength to pull us up. We have to acknowledge God our strength as the One who has brought us this far. Yes, the enemy has a plan to destroy us, but God has plans to expand and use us to destroy the enemy. No wonder the enemy is so afraid of us. No wonder he tries so hard to keep us on his side.

In Case You Didn't Know . . .
For those who do not yet have a right relationship with God, the first step is to accept the gift of God, Jesus' death on the cross, as payment for our sin and receive the power to become a child of God.

Let's broaden our perspective a bit. We must acknowledge that the same payment took care of our sins and the sins of others against us. In order to enjoy the fullness of God's forgiveness in this life, it is essential to drop the charges we have against others.

Though Jesus has paid for everybody's sin as far as God is concerned, the law of reaping and sowing is still in effect when it concerns people. When people do unjust things to others, they will reap what they sow in their bodies (Galatians 6:7-8). But as long as we hang on to those who have offended us, it makes it more difficult for them to reap what they have sowed. Accepting Christ's forgiveness for ourselves necessitates releasing others.

As African American women awaken to spiritual reality, walk in the Spirit and live in oneness with God, loving with his love, the enemy will not be allowed to continue killing, stealing and destroying our families and cities.

African American women who are members of Christ have to accept some of the responsibility for what has happened in our communities. We have played a part in allowing it. We each have the responsibility to live as godly people, to be part of the solution by allowing our bodies to be instruments in the hand of God.

There are some practical things we can do. Christians can participate in the communion table with the knowledge contained in this chapter. The next time we take communion, it would be of great benefit to ask God to give us indications of bitterness or idols in our hearts. As we become aware of false gods or bitterness, we pray the prayer of confession.

But even as we acknowledge the forgiveness of our personal sins, it would be appropriate to also acknowledge the sea of forgiveness that covers the sins of our African brothers and sisters who sold us into slavery, the slave masters in our ancestral heritage, ancestors who may have adopted a root of bitterness, parents, bosses, husbands, boyfriends and anyone who has rejected us.

We can then declare to God that we want all of the evil in our family uprooted. We can ask him for strength to cooperate with his plans of uprooting. As we tell God with his strength we desire to bless and curse not, we give him permission to do a new thing in us and to the people we influence.

Though we cannot change what has happened in the past, we can change our response to it. We have the power to stop the poison of the past from continuing to affect us today and being passed on to others.

In order to get this whole thing turned around, we first need to go to God and make things right with him. We need to admit he is not the problem. We need to acknowledge our own responsibility. We should ask God to forgive us for believing the accusations against him.

Second, we need to repent. We need to turn around in our thoughts and actions toward God and others.

Third, we have to turn from the lies that have been ingrained in our minds about God, about men and about our own worth.

Fourth, we must ask God to heal our broken hearts and to help us sense his presence and his love.

Finally, we need to release all those who have been used by the enemy to cause us pain and rejection.

Let us forget what is behind us, and let us press on. Forget it. Forget the good and the bad. This is a new day, a new beginning. The failures, the pain, the hurts of yesterday are under the blood of Jesus.

There will be times the Holy Spirit will take us to the past to undo some hooks, to release some people, to even forgive ourselves; but for right now, let's just forget the past. We could never figure it out anyway. Let's just go with a clean slate to learn a new thing.

Many would have us believe change only comes from elsewhere. Some would have us think when drug dealers, abortionists and gang members change, things will get better for our cities. But I say when African American women who are chosen vessels, keys to change, figure out their purpose in God, we will see a new day. It's time for that, my friend.

That is our destiny: African American Christian women being victorious over God's enemy, chosen vessels, keys to change in the hand of a faithful God!

Nike says, "Just do it." I say it's our time; let's just do it.

Questions for Thought and Action

1. What biblical truths refute the lie that God loves us less because we're black?

2. Why is forgiveness one key in reversing the curse?

3. How does blessing those who curse us help us reverse the curse?

4. Why is unforgiveness like housing a thief?

5. Why is a hidden rift with God such a possibility for African Americans?

6. Read Philippians 3:13-14. Why do we need to forget the good and the bad of the past and press on to the future?

7. *Going deeper:* What will you do the next time you are tempted to complain about what others have done to hold you back?

8. Take a moment now to meditate upon and pray aloud this prayer. (If you cannot pray it at this time, perhaps you will be able to at a later time.) "Father, many people have offended me. I now understand why forgiving them is important to my freedom. I choose to forgive all who have wronged me. I ask for your power now as I release (put in as many names as you need to) _____

_____

_____

_____ from their debt to me. I also ask that you not hold their sin against me to their charge."

17

it's time, our time

◆ ◆

To every thing there is a season,
a time for every purpose under the heaven.
He has made every thing beautiful in its time. Also He has put
eternity in their hearts, except that no one can find out the work that God
does from beginning to end. (ECCLESIASTES 3:1, 11)

K eys are small tools designed by God, the master key-maker. Sometimes keys are shaped in the fires of pain. Keys can be small objects, not really appearing significant, not very useful for a lot of things, but they can open a locked door. Without keys, doors remain locked and everything behind them is not available. Behind the door may lie vast riches—maybe spiritual and financial blessings, maybe emotional and physical healings.

It is time African American Christian women begin to move forth into what God has called them to be. They hold the key to the door of change in our churches and cities and healing for our nation. It is time for us to rise and take our place to facilitate God's healing in this land. It's time to humble ourselves, pray, seek God's face and turn from our wicked ways.

Are we willing to "stand in the gap" for the men and others in our lives? Are we ready to practice our warfare techniques to free them, even as we are getting free ourselves? Are we ready and willing to release the men in our life and the society in general from the offenses they have brought to us? Are we ready to break the cycles of inferiority, domination and rejection?

The power to break the cycles is in God. As we submit to God, he gives us victory.

The woman of God realizes many people, even some of her family members, need to be rescued from prisons of immorality, drugs, violence and religion, among other things. She is willing to go into these prisons, using the weapons of her warfare obtained in the fiery furnace to release those God assigns to her life.

It's time to gladly participate in a ministry of bringing deliverance to others. Women, it's time to reevaluate all we have experienced through this new understanding and come to Joseph's conclusion: although Satan meant our slavery and prison experience for evil, God meant it for good.

It's Time to Be Keys of Change

It's time to really know God as our friend. It's time to get ourselves all intertwined in Jesus, standing with him. It's time to let go of any weights that would slow us down. It's time to have our full dependency in Jesus.

It's time to be shaken out of the traditions of religion and take our place in the body of Christ. It's time to fall in love with Jesus. It's time to experience God's love for us. It's time to allow God to do some major heart surgery. It's time to be vessels of honor, fit for the Master's use (2 Timothy 2:21).

It's time to surrender all to Jesus. It's time to put everything on the altar. It's time to deny ourselves, take up our cross and follow Jesus. It's time to stop playing games and build our house on the solid rock, Jesus Christ.

It's time to refuse to be a tool in the hand of the enemy. It's time to refuse to go along with his plan. It's time to stop reacting to the people Satan uses against us by choosing to walk in the Spirit. It's time to know the identity of the real enemy. It's time to get off the enemy's side and to come all the way over to Jesus' side in radical obedience. It's time to say to Satan "enough and no more!"

Yes, we can be first. Yes, we can humble ourselves and be the first to say, "Forgive me, I've been wrong holding that against you all these years. I'll release you. Jesus died for your wrong. It's been paid for. I refuse to hold it to your charge." Even though others have been wrong in judging us by our color and gender, it's time for us to confess the wrong way we have reacted to the injustices.

It's time to admit we have not covered sins with love, nor have we prayed or cried out to God for mercy. It's time for us to do business with our Father. It's time we believe his evaluation of our worth.

It's time to know God freely forgives us for our mistake, faults, weakness and sins. It's time to be aware he's not as bothered about them as we are. It's time to be honest with God, to admit/confess those things hindering us so he can have the liberty to change us. It's time to stop denying, blaming, projecting, minimizing, rationalizing and making excuses.

It's time to experience Jesus' love, acceptance and forgiveness in spite of our past failures, weaknesses and mistakes. It's time to walk out of the prison door Jesus has already opened, away from the walls we've built up around ourselves, to freedom. Jesus is giving us that choice. It's time to take it. It's time to make change in spite of pain.

It's time to swallow our pride; it's time to stop pretending. It's time to drop the masks and expose the enemy's work in our life.

It's time to be real with ourselves, with each other and with God if the world is ever going to see Jesus in us.

It's time to stop holding our breath waiting for others to change. It's time to bring God's kingdom to our world.

It's time to regain our places as keepers of our homes and communities, creating an atmosphere of unconditional love, acceptance and forgiveness. It's time to turn away from bitterness and unforgiveness. Instead of sarcasm, criticism, gossip or slander coming from our lips, it's time to demonstrate the law of wisdom and kindness.

It's time to be godly influences to our children. It's time to cease from disciplining them out of frustration and anger, continuing negative cycles. It's time to give them the same unconditional love we all crave for. It's time to be kind and patient with them. It's time to have hope and belief in them no matter how many mistakes they have made.

It's our time to lean on Jesus, listening for his secrets and commands and feeling his heartbeat. It's our time to be told the strategy and plan for victory in battle. It's time to use the information received in our prayer closet. It's time to wage spiritual warfare.

With Jesus and his fullness in us, upon us, around us and for us, it's time we claim our complete restoration and a double refund on what the enemy has taken from us. It's time to avail ourselves of the power now at our disposal to forgive, get untangled and go forth to free others from their yokes, entanglements and prisons.

It's time to exercise authority over the plans and purposes of the enemy by staying close to our Master. It's time to be recognized by Jesus.

It is time for us to develop our relationship with our heavenly Father based on truth, not lies. Women are such potentially powerful weapons in the hand of God! We can choose to be a tool in the hand of a faithful God to smash the gates of hell and release many captives!

It's time to visit the ones caught up in the prisons of drugs, alcohol, homosexuality and prostitution. It's time to give them the good news that God loves, accepts and forgives them and can free them.

It's time to recognize that God is good. It's time to hear him say, "Well done, my good and faithful servant."

It's Our Time of Destiny

When we say that it is our time of destiny, we mean we are destined to be great in letting the captives go free. All those we have held in captivity to their wrongs against us, we now release. Instead of holding them captive, we'll now pray for, bless and do good unto them.

To those who are exposed to the enemy because of unconfessed sin, we offer "covers" of love and prophecies of comfort. To those who are hungry for unconditional love, we offer a feast at our tables of tenderness, nurture and understanding. It's time to give refreshing water of healing to the thirsty.

When we say it's our time, we're saying we'll lay down our lives in prayer until the love of God and the truth of his Word breaks through upon others. When we say it's our time, we're saying we'll take our turn at letting go of bitterness.

When we say it's our time to teach, we mean that it's time to teach others warfare techniques. It's time to teach prayer strategies. It's time to share life experiences, encouraging others.

It's time to trade pain for a destiny of glory. It's time to experience real joy. It's time to realize the depth of pain and suffering is in direct proportion to our capacity for God's joy and blessings. It's time for the deep crevices of African American women to be filled with God's presence. It's time to receive a double portion of God's power as we become clean and chosen vessels, glorifying him. God is ready to do his greatest work in and through us!

When we say it's our time, we're saying we'll seek his strength. By the grace of God, African American women can be a vital part of the most powerful display of the purposes of God this nation has ever seen.

African American women, it is our time! Let's use it to be salt and light in the world.

African American women, we hold the keys to change. Let's make it our business to use them to God's glory!

IT'S OUR TIME

To everything there is a season
To every purpose there is a time
The God who made the nations
Has everything in His hands
And He wants the world to know Him
Through His love and righteousness
And He's called us to His kingdom
For such a time as this.

Chorus
Now it's our time to believe
It's our time to love and live
There was a time to receive
Now it's time for us to give
Standing hand in hand together
Let's reach out and touch our own
Can you hear the Spirit calling
It's our time.

There was a time we were the learners
Now it's time for us to teach
There was a time for us to follow
Now it's time for us to lead
There was a time we used to borrow
Now it's time for us to feed
It's our world, it's our nation
It's our time of destiny.

We have an obligation
To reach our generation
and pray His kingdom come within our world
And I know we can succeed
Simply cause we do believe
He has given all we need
To carry on.

by Myles Munroe
(used by permission)

To contact Rebecca Osaigbovo regarding her speaking ministry write

Chosen Vessels Ministries
P.O. Box 23872
Detroit, MI 48223
Chosvessel@aol.com